** The Gate of Trust - Shaar Bitachon **

Gate #4 of Chovot Halevavot - Duties of the Heart
by Rabeinu Bahya ibn Paquda zt'l
(with commentaries)

english translation by Rabbi Yosef Sebag

copyright 2018 dafyomireview.com

SOME OTHER WORKS BY RABBI YOSEF SEBAG

Duties of the Heart   - www.dafyomireview.com/384

Path of the Just   - www.dafyomireview.com/447

Gates of Holiness   - www.dafyomireview.com/442

Marks of Divine Wisdom - www.dafyomireview.com/427

Torah Numerology   - www.dafyomireview.com/453

Torah Authenticity   - www.dafyomireview.com/447

yosefsebag@gmail.com

Dafyomi **A**dvancement **F**orum

Produced by Kollel Iyun Hadaf • Rosh Kollel: Rabbi Mordecai Kornfeld

'Your Chavrusa in Yerushalayim'

בס"ד

Rosh Kollel:
Rabbi Berel Eichenstein

Chairman of the Board:
Rabbi Gedalya Rabinowitz
Munostrishtcher Rebbe

Advisory Board:
Rabbi Berel Eichenstein
Rabbi Aharon Feldman
Rabbi Emanuel Feldman
Rabbi Yaakov I. Homnick
Rabbi Zecharyah Greenwald
Rabbi Elimelech Kornfeld
Rabbi Joseph Pearlman
Rabbi Fabian Schonfeld
Rabbi Berel Wein
Rabbi Chaim Wilschanski
Dr. Moshe Snow
Dr. Eli Turkel
Avi Berger
Samson Krupnick ל"ז
Andrew Neff
Mordechai Rabin, LLM
Kenneth Spetner ל"ז
Uri Wolfson

Talmud-study publications:
In English:
Insights to the Daf
Background to the Daf
Dafyomi Review Q & A
Outlines of the Daf
Halachah Outlines for the Daf
Ask the Kollel (email/fax)
Weekly In-Depth Video Lectures
Daily Quizzes on the Daf
Mishnah Yomis Review Q & A
Revach l'Daf

בעברית:
יוסף דעת (הערות)
יוסף דעת (שאלות לחזרת)
גלי מסכתא (סיכומי סוגיות)
טבלאות לכל דף
חידוני חזרה

Bookmarks & Calendars

Leather-bound 12th-cycle calendar
Yearly Dafyomi-schedule bookmarks
Dafyomi-cycle bookmarks
Rishonim-on-the-Shas bookmarks
Hadran cards

Chovos ha'Levavos, the monumental work of Rabeinu Bachye ben Yosef Ibn Pakuda, a judge in Islamic Spain (circa 1040), is one of the earliest works on Jewish philosophy and beliefs. It remains one of the fundamental works of Musar and Hashkafah. Even the great Rambam (Maimonides) bases a large part of his treatises in these fields on the revered words of the Chovos ha'Levavos. (It has been suggested that Rav Shlomo Ibn Gevirol took ideas from the Chovos ha'Levavos as well.)

Originally written in Arabic, this classic was translated into Hebrew not longer after its original publication, and more recently to many other languages. Among works of Jewish philosophy, its prominence in even the most traditional houses of learning makes it unique. The Chovos ha'Levavos' methodical and systematic analyses or every aspect of the human character makes reading it an experience in growth through introspection.

We owe a debt of gratitude to Rabbi Yosef Sebag for his exceptionally readable English translation of this important work. By adding translations of classic commentaries on the text, he has made the depth of the work available to all. Rabbi Sebag's investment of time and effort is evident in every part of the work, but especially in the Sha'ar ha'Yichud, the somewhat "controversial" section dealing with philosophical proofs of G-d.

I have known Rabbi Sebag for many years, and I have witnessed firsthand his overwhelming dedication to Torah-study and to raising a family on Torah-true ideals. His careful adherence to the instructions of our Torah giants, coupled with his strong will to teach others the timeless lessons of the Torah, has made him a true "Ben Aliyah."

May his investment bear the dividends of allowing him to help many of our brethren improve their faith and strength of character!

With Torah blessings,

Rabbi Mordecai Kornfeld

Israel office: P.O.B. 43087, Jerusalem 91430, Israel • US office: 140-32 69 Ave., Flushing, NY 11367
Tel. - Israel: (02) 651-5004 • Fax - Israel: (02) 591-6024 • email: daf@dafyomi.co.il
http://www.dafyomi.co.il • http://dafyomi.shemayisrael.co.il/
U.S. tax ID: 11-3354586   580-28-908-0 ע"ר מסי

Original Hebrew at end of book

Free Online Version at
www.dafyomireview.com/380

** The Gate of Trust - Shaar HaBitachon **

from Chovos Halevavos - Duties of the Heart

by Rabeinu Bahya ibn Paquda

(With Select Classic Commentaries)
translated by Rabbi Yosef Sebag
copyright 2020 dafyomireview.com - All rights are reserved

Translator's Foreword :
The following is a translation of the fourth gate of one of the earliest of the classic mussar works, Chovos Halevavos by Rabeinu Bahya. The book has inspired many great men to walk in its ways and review it throughout their lives. The fourth gate deals with what Rabeinu Bachya regards as "the most necessary of all things for the service of G-d."

I have found that the gate must be read in its entirety otherwise one will not have understood anything properly. In this second revision, I added select commentaries and also checked/compared every sentence against the brilliant translation by Rabbi Moses Hyamson O.B.M., the former chief Rabbi and head Dayan of England between 1911 and 1913. The translator studied in various yeshivas under great Torah scholars such as Rabbi Dov Shwartzman zt'l (~2 years), Rabbi Nachman Bulman zt'l, Rabbi Nissan Kaplan (~5 years). He also completed a degree in physics at the University of Massachusetts, Amherst and was a research associate in nuclear physics for a few years before heading off to yeshiva.

- Yosef Sebag, Jerusalem Tishrei 5775/ Oct 2014

Abbreviations used in this translation:
MH - **Manoach HeLevavos commentary by Rabbi Manoach Hendel (1540-1611)**
TL - **Tov HaLevanon commentary by Rabbi Yisrael Halevi (1700-1777)**
PL - **Pas Lechem commentary by Rabbi Chaim Avraham Hacohen (1740-1815)**
ML - **Marpe Lenefesh commentary by Rabbi Refael Mendel (1825-1895)**
LT - **Lev Tov commentary by Rabbi Pinchas Lieberman (1929-2005)**
MC - **Matanas Chelko commentary by Rabbi Mattisyahu Solomon (with permission)**

from Chovos Halevavos - Duties of the Heart
by Rabeinu Bachye zt'l

Introduction

The author says: Since our previous treatise dealt with the duty to assume the service of G-d, I deemed proper to follow it with what is more necessary than all other things for one who serves G-d - placing one's trust in Him for all matters, the reason being the great benefits this yields both in religious and in secular matters.

The benefits in religious matters:

Among them, peace of mind, and trusting in G-d as a servant must trust in his master. Because if one does not place his trust in G-d, he will place his trust in something else. And whoever trusts in something other than G-d, the Al-mighty will remove His providence from such a person, and leave him in the hands of the one he trusted. And he will be as it was written: *"For My people have committed two evils; they have forsaken Me, the spring of living waters, to dig for themselves cisterns, broken cisterns that do not hold water"* (Yirmiya 2:13), *"They exchanged their Glory for the likeness of an ox eating grass"* (Tehilim 106:20), *"Blessed is the man who trusts in the L-ord; the L-ord shall be his refuge"* (Yirmiya 17:7), *"Praiseworthy is the man who made the L-ord his trust, and did not turn to the haughty and those who turn to falsehood."* (Tehilim 40:5), *"Cursed is the man who trusts in man, who makes flesh his strength and whose heart turns away from the L-ord"* (Yirmiya 17:5).

(*Matanas Chelko*: *"if one does not place his trust in G-d, he will place his trust in something else...they have forsaken Me"* - this is a great fundamental principle, namely, that every person trusts his life in something or someone. One who claims he does not trust in anything [unless he is 100% sure] is fooling himself. Since this is the way of the world. A man who purchases a loaf of bread from the baker trusts that no poison was placed there. If he takes his automobile to the mechanic for repair and afterwards drives it on the highway, he trusts that it was repaired properly. Likewise for trusting his life with the doctors and other similar matters. Hence, one who trusts in these things cannot say "I cannot trust in G-d

until I fully understand everything and fully see everything".
This is false! For behold, he trusts his life on many things
and many human beings without fully knowing all that
happened.)

If he places his trust in his wisdom and tactics, physical strength
and industriousness - he will toil for nothing, his strength will
weaken, and his tactics will fall short of accomplishing his desire,
as written *"He traps the wise with their own cunning"* (Iyov 5:13)
(that their tactics result in bad instead of good - *TL*), and *"I
returned and saw under the sun, that the race does not belong to
the swift, nor the battle to the mighty; neither do the wise have
bread, [nor do the understanding have wealth, nor the
knowledgeable favor, for time and chance happens to them all]"*
(Koheles 9:11), and *"Young lions suffer want and are hungry, but
those who seek the L-ord lack no good"* (Tehilim 34:11).

(*Matanas Chelko*: *"whoever trusts in something other than
G-d...the Almighty will leave him"* - i.e. that he places his
trust (hope/peace of mind) on the country or on the alarm
system in his home, or the like of the various cause and
effect calculations. There are grounds for a claim against him
for he does trust on things, just not on the Master of the
world. His punishment is that G-d leaves him to "nature" and
to the framework to which he placed his trust. Therefore, he
is ruled over by that system of nature, with its many statistics
of causes and effects. Hence, he who thinks his own
strength and ingenuity earned for him all of his success, and
he relies on this, G-d will leave him under that system of
causes and effects. Through this, certainly he will eventually
stumble and be lost. [because: "the race is not to the swift,
nor the battle to the strong...."]

If he relies on his wealth, it will be removed from him and left to
someone else as written *"He lies down rich, but there shall be
nothing to gather; he opens his eyes, and his wealth is not"* (Iyov
27:19), *"Do not weary yourself to grow rich; cease from your own
understanding."* (Mishlei 23:4), *"Should you blink your eyes at it,
it is not here; for it will make wings for itself, like the eagle, and it
will fly toward the heavens."* (Mishlei 23:5), *"so it is he who
gathers riches but not by right; he shall leave them in the midst of*

his days, and at his end he stands dishonored" (Yirmiya 17:11) (since if he placed all of his trust on his riches, certainly, he will not be clean from various forms of theft and dishonesty - *PL*)

Or, he will be prevented from its benefit as the wise man said *"the Al-mighty will not give him the ability to eat from it"* (Koheles 6:2), and it will be by him like a deposit that he guards from damages until it reaches someone worthy of it, as written *"[For to a man who is good in His sight, He has given wisdom and knowledge and joy,] but to the sinner He has given an occupation to gather and to accumulate, to give to him who is good in G-d's sight; this too is vanity and frustration."* (Koheles 2:26), and *"he will prepare, but a righteous man will wear them; and the pure shall divide the silver"* (Iyov 27:17). And it is possible that the money will be the cause of his destruction *(in this world) and ultimate downfall (in the afterlife)* as written *"There is a grievous evil that I saw under the sun; riches kept by their owner for his harm."* (Koheles 5:12).

(*Matanas Chelko*: A person thinks that if he attains great wealth, he will be free of worries. The truth is that it is not so. For example, a very wealthy man may be in constant worry and fear that his children will be kidnapped for ransom. Hence, his wealth has become the cause of his worry. For due to it, he is in fear of bad people. If he attains great wealth, he will see that he cannot trust in it and worries about potential mishaps. His days are squandered in worry and vexation. But he who trusts in G-d and prays to him at every step, and thanks Him for whatever he attains, then even if G-d bestows great wealth to him, he still stays with his trust and does not worry on account of his wealth. For, he never relied on himself, not before he became rich nor afterwards. While he who relies on his strength and ingenuity, and thinks the world works solely through causes and effects. Over time, he will be filled with worries and fears of many things. This itself is a punishment. It is possible also that he will be punished more severely than this, namely, that G-d will take away his wealth and he will not benefit from all his labor. Or even worse, that the wealth will be the cause of his evil as before (that his children are kidnapped for ransom or the like.)

Another benefit for the one who trusts in the Al-mighty, is that his trust will lead him to the following:

* to not serve other than G-d.
* to not hope in any man, nor expect from anyone (Micha 5:6).
* to not work to win their approval.
* to not flatter them.
* to not agree with them in what is not the service of G-d (ex. going to their time wasting parties - PL).
* to not be afraid of their matters.
* to not be afraid of disagreeing with them (of not conforming to their ways - PL; "to not be afraid if they quarrel with him and outcast him" - ML).
* to divest himself of the cloak of their favors and free himself from the burden of expressing gratitude to them, and from the obligation of paying back their favors (and therefore he will not need to flatter them, or join them in what is not the service of G-d - TL).

> (*Marpe Lenefesh*: He endeavors and does everything he can to not need others and to not enclothe himself in the favors of others. For this would place him under an obligation to toil to express gratitude to them and to also make a return, as it is proper and obligatory to pay back a benefactor with good, as mentioned earlier in the beginning of the third gate. Rather, he desires that G-d alone be his benefactor and that he thanks only Him.)

* if he rebukes them, he will not be afraid of slighting them.
* he will not shy from humiliating them (so that his rebuke is effective - PL).
* he will not embellish their false ways (to them, but rather will denigrate it to them - PL)

As the prophet wrote: "*But the L-ord G-d helps me, therefore shall I not be confounded; therefore have I set my face like a flint, and I know that I shall not be ashamed*" (Yeshaya 50:7), "*Do not fear them or their words*" (Yechezkel 2:6), "*And you, son of man, fear them not, and fear not their words*" (Yechezkel 2:6), "*fear them not, neither shall you be intimidated by them*" (Yechezkel 3:9).

Another benefit: The trust in G-d will lead one to empty his mind from the distractions of the world, and to focus his heart to matters of service of G-d.

> (*Marpe Lenefesh*: This is because the chief cause of mental agitation and confusion which prevents a man from learning torah and devoting himself to religious service is - constant worry on his livelihood, how will he earn money and through what means. But one who trusts in G-d will diminish his worry in this and increase his worry for religious service. And he will have tranquility of heart like the Alchemist, and even more...)

And he will be similar in his peace of mind, tranquility of heart, and few financial worries to the alchemist, one who knows how to transform silver to gold and copper or tin to silver through skill and procedures.

> (*Pas Lechem*: the author used this trade as an example because many of the masses of his generation aspired to it, due to its making great wealth.
> Translator: In our times it is much easier to detect fake gold and so the trade has lost its appeal. Perhaps a modern day analogy of the alchemist would be one who owns a sophisticated counterfeit money machine.)

And the one who trusts in G-d will have the following 10 advantages over the alchemist:

(1) The alchemist requires special materials to perform his operation, without which he cannot do anything. These materials are not found at all times and in all places. But for one who trusts in G-d, his sustenance is assured and can come through any means of all the means of the world, as written *"[And He fed you with manna, which you knew not, neither did your fathers know]; That He might make known to you that man does not live by bread alone..."* (Devarim 8:3). For at no time and in no place are the means of obtaining his livelihood withheld from him, as you know already from the story of Eliyahu and the ravens, or with the widow and the cakes and water (Melachim 17:9), or the story of Ovadia with the prophets, where he said *"I hid among the*

prophets of G-d, 100 men, 50 in each cave, and I fed them bread and water" (Melachim 18:13) (i.e. Ovadia was a means to provide for the prophets - *PL*), and *"Young lions suffer want and are hungry, but those who seek the L-ord lack no good"* (Tehilim 34:11), and *"Fear the L-ord, His holy ones; for there is no want to those who fear Him"* (Tehilim 34:10).

(2) The alchemist must perform actions and follow procedures without which he cannot successfully complete his goal. It is even possible that the fumes and odors will cause his death, along with the long work and great effort with them day and night. But one who trusts in G-d is secure against mishaps, and his heart is assured against future (potential) bad things. Whatever comes to him from G-d, he will accept with joy and gladness and his livelihood comes to him peacefully, quietly, and happily, as written *"He causes me to lie down in green pastures; He leads me beside still waters"* (Tehilim 23:2).

> (*Pas Lechem commentary*: "whatever comes to him from G-d gives him joy..." is an explanation of the previous statement "his heart is assured against bad things..." because certainly it cannot be taken literally, that for one who trusts in G-d, no bad things will ever happen to him. For what our eyes see contradicts this. Rather, after he trusts in G-d that He will not do to him anything that is not for his good, if so, "whatever comes to him from G-d, he will accept with joy and gladness", as the Talmud says in Berachot 54a. Therefore it is correct to say that no bad things ever happen to him.
>
> Translator: Later on in Gate #8 he says: "And when you do this (spiritual accounting) with a faithful heart and a pure soul, your mind will become illuminated, and you will see the path to all of the exalted qualities... and you will reach the status of one treasured by G-d... You will not part from a permanent joy in this world and in the next..." see there.)

(3) The alchemist does not trust anyone with his secret due to fear for his life. But one who trusts G-d does not fear any man on account of his trust. On the contrary, it is a source of honor, as

king David said: *"in G-d I trusted, I will not fear, what can a man do to me?"* (Tehilim 54:12).

(4) The alchemist must either prepare one large quantity of gold and silver for long term needs or must prepare small batches for short term needs.

If he prepares a large quantity, all his days he will fear for his life that perhaps all the gold and silver will be lost in any number of ways (and he will be left penniless), and his heart will never quiet, nor will his mind be at peace due to fear of the king and of the people (finding his big stash of gold).

If he makes small batches for short term use, it is possible that he will not successfully perform the procedure at a time of great need, due to a failure in one of the means.

> (*Matanas Chelko*: i.e. even if he is successful, he is in a constant state of worry. Likewise, in our times, we can observe that anyone who is successful in business is also worried about many factors - unless he trusts in G-d. Hence he is just like the Alchemist.)

But one who trusts in G-d, has strong peace of mind that G-d will provide for him at any time He wishes and in any place, just like He sustains the fetus in its mother's womb or the chick inside an egg, which has no opening to enter anything from the outside, and birds in the air, or fish in the sea, and the tiny ant despite its weakness, while the mighty lion some days cannot obtain food, as written *"Young lions suffer want and are hungry, but those who seek the L-ord lack no good"* (Tehilim 34:11). And *"The L-ord will not starve the soul of the righteous"* (Mishlei 10:3), and *"I have been young, and now am old; yet I have not seen the righteous forsaken, nor his seed begging bread"* (Tehilim 37:25).

> (*Translator*: "Young lions suffer want..." - notice dear reader that this verse was brought three times already. Perhaps, the intent is to teach one to repeat such verses to himself whenever he can as a way of working on trust.)

(5) The alchemist is under anxiety and fear of everyone, from the greatest to the lowest of people as a consequence of his work,

but one who trusts in G-d will be revered by great men and honorable people, even animals and stones seek to do his will (i.e. do not harm him - TL) as written in the entire Psalm *"He who sits..."* (Tehilim 91), and *"In six troubles He will save you, and in the seventh no harm will touch you."* (Job 5:19), until the end of the matter.

(6) The alchemist is not immune from sickness and disease which hinders his joy in being wealthy, and prevents him from benefiting from what he has and enjoying what he has acquired. But one who trusts in G-d, is immune from sickness and disease except as an atonement or to increase his reward, as written *"Now youths shall become tired and weary, and young men shall stumble"* (Isaiah 40:30), *"those who hope in G-d will renew strength"* (Isaiah 40:31), and *"for the arms of the wicked (who trust in their strength - TL) shall be broken, but the L-ord supports the righteous"* (Tehilim 37:17).

(7) It is possible that the alchemist will not be able to buy food with his gold and silver due to no food being available in the city at times, as written: *"they shall cast their money in the streets"* (Ezekiel 7:19), and *"neither silver nor gold will be able to save them"* (Tzefania 1:18). But for one who trusts in G-d, his sustenance will not be blocked at any time or in any place, as written: *"in famine He redeemed you from death"* (Job 5:20), and *"the L-ord is my shepherd, I shall not lack"* (Tehilim 23:1), and *"They will not be shamed in time of calamity, and in days of famine they shall still be satisfied"* (Tehilim 37:19).

(8) The alchemist does not linger in one place too long due to fear that his secret will be discovered. But one who trusts in G-d feels secure in his land and has peace of mind in his place, as written *"Trust in the L-ord and do good; dwell in the land and be nourished by faith"* (Tehilim 37:3), and *"The righteous shall inherit the land and dwell forever in it"* (Tehilim 37:29).

(9) The alchemist's skills will not accompany him in the afterlife. They may only provide him, in this world, security from poverty and from needing other people. But for one who trusts in G-d, the reward for his trust will accompany him in this world and in the

next, as written *"Many are the pains of the wicked (in the afterlife - PL); but one who trusts in G-d will be surrounded by kindness"* (Tehilim 32:10), and *"how great is Your goodness that you hid away for those who fear You"* (Tehilim 31:20).

> (*Tov Halevanon*: He will receive reward for his trust in G-d in the afterlife since placing one's trust in G-d is a big mitzvah, as written (Bereishit 15:10): *"And Avraham believed in the L-ord; and He counted it to him as a righteousness".*)

(10) If the alchemist's work is discovered, it will become a cause for his death, because his work runs contrary to the natural order, and the Director of the world will allow someone to kill him when he fails to hide his secret (G-d won't save him at a time of danger. Alternatively, G-d will cause him to be caught when his time has come - *ML*). But for one who trusts in G-d, when his trust becomes known, he will be held in high esteem and honored by the public. They will feel blessed to be near him or to see him, and his presence will bring good fortune to the city and shield the people from troubles, as written: *"the righteous man is the foundation of the world"* (Mishlei 10:25), similar to Lot in Tzoar (Bereishit 19, who saved the city by his presence there - *TL*).

Among the benefits of trusting in G-d regarding religious matters: One who trusts in G-d, if he has wealth, will be quick to fulfill his monetary obligations to G-d and to men with a willing and generous spirit. If he does not have wealth, he will consider that lack of wealth to be among the favors of G-d to him, because he is exempt from the monetary obligations to G-d and men which wealth brings, and he is spared from the mental distraction of protecting and managing it, as one of the pious used to say: "may G-d save me from dispersion of the mind". They would ask him "what is dispersion of the mind?" He would answer: "to own property at the head of every river and the center of every town." And this is what our sages referred to in saying: *"the more possessions, the more worry"* (Avos 2:7), and they said: *"who is wealthy? He who is content with what he has"* (Avos 4:1).

One who trusts in G-d will receive the benefits of money, namely, his material needs, but without the mental distraction and constant worry of the wealthy, as the wise man said *"The sleep of the laborer is sweet, whether he eats little or much, but the satiety of the rich does not allow him to sleep"* (Koheles 5:11).

Another benefit, one who trusts in G-d will not diminish his trust on account of having much wealth because he does not rely on the money. He regards it as a deposit which he is ordered to use in specific ways, for specific matters and for a limited time. And if he stays wealthy for a long time, he will not become arrogant due to his wealth. He will not remind the poor person of his charity gifts since he was commanded to give to him, and he will not seek his gratitude and praises. Rather, he will thank his Creator who appointed him as a means for doing good to the poor person.

If his wealth is lost, he will not worry nor mourn his loss. Rather, he will thank his Creator for taking back His deposit, just like he thanked G-d when it was given to him. He will be happy with his portion, and will not seek to damage others (in order to gain benefit - *TL*). He will not covet other people's wealth as the wise man said *"A righteous man eats to sate his appetite, [but the stomach of the wicked shall feel want]."* (Mishlei 13:25).

(*Matanas Chelko*: This is analogous to a case of two poor neighbors. One of whom had a rich relative who came to visit him and gave him a huge donation of 1000 dollars and then left. Upon hearing about the donation, the second neighbor begged his friend for 200 dollars but he refused. The neighbor pleaded for 100 dollars and this time his friend painfully agreed. But if from the beginning, the rich relative said to him, "I see you and your neighbor are both in great poverty. Take 800 dollars for yourself and take an additional 200 for your neighbor". Surely, he would have ran joyously to his neighbor without sadness or heavy feeling. This is because he never felt like the owner of that 200.. So too, one who has money beyond his needs must feel that it is not only for himself but for distributing also to others. Hence, one who trusts in G-d is always joyful in all situations for he knows and feels this secret.

Benefits of trust in G-d for worldly matters:

* Peace of mind from the worries of this world.

* Peace from the frenzy and drive to pursue the lusts of this world.

* Feeling calm, secure, at peace in this world, as written *"blessed be the man who trusts in G-d, and G-d shall be his refuge"* (Yirmiyahu 17:7), and *"For he shall be like a tree planted by the water, that sends out its roots by the stream. [It does not fear when heat comes; its leaves stay green. It has no worries in a year of drought and shall not cease to bear fruit]"* (Yirmiyahu 17:8).

Among them, peace of mind from the need to travel to faraway journeys, which weakens the body, and hastens aging, as written *"my strength has weakened from the journey, my life shortened"* (Tehilim 102:24).

It is said about a novice ascetic who travelled to a distant land in search of a livelihood. He met one of the idolaters of the city where he arrived and said to him: "how completely blind and ignorant you are to worship idols!". The idolater asked him: "And what do you worship?". The ascetic answered "I worship the Creator, the Omnipotent, the Sustainer of all, the One, the Provider of all, which there is none like Him". The idolater countered "your actions contradict your words!" The ascetic asked "How so?", the idolater said "if what you say were true, He would have provided a livelihood for you in your own city, just like He provided for you here, and it would not have been necessary for you to trouble yourself to travel to a faraway land like this." The ascetic, unable to answer, returned to his city and reassumed his asceticism from that time on, and never again left his city (for his livelihood).

Another benefit, peace of mind and body, due to sparing oneself from pursuing grueling jobs, and wearying occupations, avoiding work of kings - mingling in their culture and dealing with their corrupt servants.

But one who trusts G-d, selects among the different occupations one which is easy on his body, allows him to earn a good reputation, does not consume his mind, and is best suited for fulfilling his torah obligations and the principles of his faith. Because the choice of occupation will neither increase nor decrease the income he will earn unless G-d decreed so, as it says *"For it is not from the east nor from the west, neither from the desert does elevation come. But G-d judges; He lowers this one and elevates that one."* (Tehilim 75:7), and *"He causes me to lie down in green pastures; He leads me beside still waters"* (Tehilim 23:2).

Another benefit, minimal aggravation in one's business dealings. If one's merchandise does not sell, or if he is unable to collect his debts, or if he is struck by illness, [he will not worry] because he knows that the Creator is in charge of his life and knows best what is good for him, as written *"Only to G-d should you hope, my soul, for my hope is from Him"* (Tehilim 62:6).

Another benefit, joy in whatever happens to him, even if it is something difficult and against his nature. Because he trusts that G-d will do only what is good for him in all matters, just like a mother has compassion on her baby in washing it, diapering it, and harnessing or unharnessing it against its will, as David said: *"Surely I have behaved and quieted myself, as a child that is weaned of his mother: my soul is even as a weaned child"* (Tehilim 131:2).

> (*Matanas Chelko*: This is the essence of trust - to feel like a baby in the hands of its mother. One should contemplate this matter of bathing the baby. The mother needs to do all sorts of things in order to cleanse it. And even though the baby does not sense the good in these things, nevertheless, the mother must do them since she knows it is for the baby's benefit. This is the conduct of G-d towards us, like a mother with her baby. All that He does and metes out to us is only for our good.

Since I have clarified the benefits of trust in G-d for religious and secular matters, I will now clarify seven topics on the matter of trust:

THE SEVEN CHAPTERS OF THE GATE OF TRUST

(1) What is trust.

(2) The criteria for trusting someone.

(3) The prerequisites to trusting in G-d.

(4) When trust applies and when it does not.

(5) The difference between one who trusts in G-d in earning a livelihood and one who does not.

(6) Obligation to refute those who promote delaying the service of G-d until reaching sufficient material prosperity.

(7) Things that damage one's trust in G-d, and a summary of the matter of trust.

*** CHAPTER 1 ***

What is trust?
Peace of mind of the one who trusts. That one relies in his heart that the one he trusts in will do what is good and proper for him on the matter he has trusted him with according to his ability and his understanding of what will further his good.

But the main factor which leads one to trust in the one trusted, and without which trust cannot exist, is for one's heart to be confident that the one trusted will keep his word and will do what he pledged, and that he will also think to do what is good for him even on what he did not pledge out of pure generosity and kindness (this will be explained).

*** CHAPTER 2 ***
- The criteria for trusting someone

CRITERIA FOR TRUSTING ONESELF IN ANOTHER
There are seven factors which make it possible for one to trust in another:

(1) Compassion, pity and love. When a man knows that his friend has compassion and pity for him, he will trust in him and be at peace with regard to troubling him with all of his matters.

(2) To know that his friend, besides loving him, is not forgetful or lazy in taking care of his needs. Rather, he knows that his friend is active and resolved to do it. Because if all of this is not clear, one's trust in him will not be complete, since one knows of his forgetfulness and laziness in attending to his needs.
But, when the one he trusts combines these two traits, great compassion for him and full attendance to his matters, he will trust in him without a doubt.

(3) He is strong. He will not be defeated in whatever he desires, and nothing can prevent him from doing the request of the one who trusts him. Because if he is weak, one cannot fully trust in him, even though it is clear that he is compassionate and active, due to the many occasions in which he failed doing things. When one combines these three traits, trusting in him will be more fitting.

(4) That the one he trusts knows what is beneficial for him, both for his inner and outer life and also that none of the ways which benefit him or further his welfare are hidden to him. Because, if he does not know all of this, one will not be at peace in entrusting himself to him. But if he combines the knowledge of the ways which are beneficial to him, the ability to implement them, great attendance to them, and compassion for him, his trust will certainly be strengthened.

(5) That the one he trusts is under the exclusive care of him from the beginning of his existence, his development, babyhood, childhood, youth, adulthood, old age until the end of his days (i.e. that no one else has ever done to him any good except the one

he trusts - *ML*). And when all this is clear to the truster, he is obligated to be at peace on his friend, and to rely on him, because of the many past benefits he already received from his friend and the constant favors he still presently receives. And this will obligate strengthening one's trust in him. (since he has been continuously benevolent to him from then until now, certainly he will not abandon him until his final end - *PL*.)

(6) All matters of the truster are entirely in the hands of the one he trusts, and no one else can hurt him, help him, benefit him, or protect him from harm, as a slave chained down in a prison is entirely in the hands of his master. If the truster were in the hands of the one he trusts in this manner, it would be more fitting to trust in him.

(*Pas Lechem*: The fifth condition was that no one else ever benefited him. This sixth condition refers to ability - that the ability to benefit or harm him is only in his friend's hands. No one else has any ability to benefit or harm him... since this is the case, his heart will not look towards trusting others and he will place all of his trust on his friend.)

(7) That the person he trusts is absolutely generous and kind (i.e. the most possible extreme of generosity and kindness - *TL*) to those deserving and to those who are not deserving, and that his generosity and kindness is continuous, never ending and without interruption.

(*Marpe Lenefesh commentary*: Otherwise, he will abandon hope from the favors of G-d, since he is in doubt whether he is worthy of them, and his trust in G-d will diminish. And through this, he will distance from G-d and His torah. Rather, let him reflect that G-d is benevolent to the good and the bad, as written: "His mercy is on all of His creations" (Tehilim 145:9). And through this, he will come closer to G-d and repent and he will become worthy of the good.)

Whoever combines these traits, in addition to all of the previous traits has completed all the conditions that deserve trust, and would obligate the person who knows this to trust in him, to be at peace internally and externally, in his heart and in his limbs, and to give himself up to him and accept his decrees and judge him favorably in all his judgments and actions. (to assume that certainly everything is good and even what seems bad is actually good - *ML*)

When we investigate these seven conditions, we will not find them at all in the created beings, but we find them all in the Creator. He is compassionate to His creations as written *"The L-ord is merciful and gracious"* (Tehilim 103:8), and *"Now should I not take pity on Nineveh, the great city"* (Yonah 4:11).

> (*Pas Lechem*: One may think that He is only merciful on those who are already in pain, but not before this, and therefore trust in Him will not help to be saved from future troubles. Therefore, the author brought the second verse from Nineveh, where G-d had pity on them even before the troubles came and annulled the decree...)

And that He never neglects us, as written *"Behold the Guardian of Israel will neither slumber nor sleep"* (Tehilim 121:4), that He is all-wise and invincible as written *"He is wise in heart and mighty in strength; who hardened [his heart] against Him and remained unhurt?"* (Job 9:4), and *"Yours, O L-ord, are the greatness, and the power, and the glory, and the victory, and the majesty"* (Divrei Hayamim I 29:11) and *"The L-ord your G-d is in your midst - a Mighty One Who will save"* (Tzefania 3:17).

And that He alone is the one who guides a person from the beginning of his existence and development, as written *"is He not your Father who has acquired you? He has made you and established you."* (Devarim 32:6), and *"by You have I been upheld from birth: You are He that took me out of my mother's womb"* (Tehilim 71:6), and *"did You not pour me out like milk and curdle me like cheese?"* (Job 10:10), and the rest of the matter.

That one's benefit or harm is not in the hands of people but rather, only in the hands of the Creator, as written *"Who has commanded and it came to pass, unless the L-ord ordained it? Out of the mouth of G-d, evil and good do not go out* (of the boundary He has set - *PL*)?"* (Eicha 3:37), and *"[All flesh is like* grass, and all their kindness is as the flower of the field]; The grass shall dry out, the flower shall wilt, but the word of our G-d will stand forever" (Isaiah 40:8), and "...surely the people are like grass" (Isaiah 40:7), and we have already explained this sufficiently in the third gate of this book.

(*Pas Lechem*: (summary) First verse shows that decrees of G-d, whether for good or for bad, do not go out of the boundaries He has decreed, rather as He decreed - so shall it be.
Second verse: Perhaps one will think that only the beginning of the matter is from G-d, but it will not endure unless a man completes it and perpetuates it, therefore - "the grass shall dry out", i.e. every man, just like his existence is ephemeral, as he is like grass, which wilts and dies, so too the kindness man does is like a temporary flower, which passes but the "word of G-d will stand forever", i.e. just like He is eternal, so too His decrees and acts are eternal.)

That His generosity is universal and His kindness is all-embracing, as written "The L-ord is good to all, and His mercies are on all His works" (Tehilim 145:9) and "Who gives food to all flesh, for His kindness endures forever" (Tehilim 136:25), and "You open Your hand and satisfy every living thing [with] will (i.e. the good He bestows is not in a stingy way, according to basic need, but rather like His will - PL)" (Tehilim 145:16).

But really, the intellect can infer that these 7 conditions exist in the Creator and not in the created beings (as he will explain next chapter - TL), and therefore I have brought these verses from scripture only as a remembrance.

(*Pas Lechem*: i.e. my intent was not as a proof otherwise I would have brought more verses, but rather only as a remembrance, namely, when these verses are constantly on a person's mouth - he will remember the 7 factors through them.

Translator: As the author wrote in the beginning of Gate #1: "that habitually having them on one's tongue always, brings one to *remembrance* of the heart...", see there)

When one clarifies this to himself, and his recognition in the true kindness of the Creator will be strong - he will place his trust in Him, give himself up completely to Him, and leave the guidance of his life to Him, never suspect Him in His judgments, nor be upset by what He has chosen for him, as David said (on the good - *TL*) *"I will lift up the cup of salvation and call upon the Name of the L-ord"* (Tehilim 116:13), and (on the bad - *TL*) *"I found trouble and sorrow and call upon the Name of the L-ord"* (Tehilim 116:3-4).

(*Pas Lechem commentary*: He first stated two general phrases:
(1) "he will place his trust in Him" - for providing his needs.
(2) "give himself up completely to Him" - this refers to a general consent and acceptance that G-d will do with him as He wishes, even for what appears bad to him.
Then he explained the two phrases:
* "and leave the guidance of his life to Him" is an explanation of (1).
* "never suspect Him in His judgments, nor be upset by what He has chosen for him" is an explanation of (2).
This latter subdivides to:
(a) "never suspect Him in His judgments" - if G-d sentences him to some bad trouble which is specific and short term.
(b) "nor be upset by what He has chosen for him" - if G-d chooses for him a widespread life-long matter such as poverty or a bad wife, or the like.)

*** **Chapter 3** ***
- *the preliminaries to trusting in G-d* -

The introductions which must be clearly understood and the truth of which must be realized in order that a person's trust in G-d will be complete are five.

> (*Pas Lechem*: When he understands them to their full depth and after this he verifies the truth of them in his heart to absolute truthfulness - then his trust in G-d will be complete)

FIRST INTRODUCTION TO BRING COMPLETE TRUST
To believe and clearly understand that all of the seven factors (in the previous chapter) which when combined make it possible to trust in someone apply to G-d. I have already mentioned them and commented on them from verses that occurred to me.
THE SEVEN FACTORS AS THEY APPLY TO G-D
One: the Creator is merciful on a man more than any other merciful being, and all mercy and compassion that a man is shown from anyone besides G-d is really derived from G-d's mercy and compassion, as the verse says "He will give you compassion, and cause others to have compassion on you and multiply you" (Devarim 13:18).

> (*Tov Halevanon*: i.e. even that which a person finds favor and compassion in the eyes of another human being - this is due to G-d's giving the person compassion on that human being towards him.
>
> *Matanas Chelko* - for example, a man walks on the street and sees a poor man. He feels compassion for him and gives him what he needs. From where did this compassion come from? From the Master of the world. On his own, the man would have kept walking and ignored the poor man. And even if he had stopped briefly and helped him a little bit, he would not have done so properly. But since G-d has compassion on the poor man, He imparts of His compassion on this man so that the man will feel compassion for the poor man. Hence, since the compassion stems from G-d, it is ascribed to G-d alone. This is the meaning of *"there is nothing but Him"* (Deut. 4:35), there is nothing in the world

| but G-d.

Two: none of the ways which benefit a man are unknown to the Creator. Logic necessitates this, since man is one of His handiworks. No one can know better than man's Maker the ways to further his making (i.e. biological conception in the womb - *PL*), and the ways of loss (where no conception will occur and the drop of human seed will be lost - *PL*), and the possible damages which can occur (in the development of the embryo in the womb during the time of pregnancy - *PL*), and the ways it (the born child during his growth and development - *PL*) can become sick and healed.

And this is also true for human makers (who know best what damages or benefits their inventions), although they do not really create anything new, but rather merely make a new form from existing raw materials, since to create a new form from nothing is impossible to man.

And all the more so, He who has called into existence from nothing the basic elements of man, his form, his anatomy, and the order of his synthesis (of body and soul - *PL*). Obviously, He is the wise One who undoubtedly knows which matters benefit or harm man in this world and in the next, as written *"I am the L-rd your G-d who teaches you for your benefit, who guides you in the proper path"* (Isaiah 48:17), and also *"G-d rebukes the ones He loves (to turn them to the proper path - TL), and like a father to a son He desires in"* (Mishlei 3:12).

Three: the Creator is the strongest of all the strong. His word reigns supreme and nothing can reverse His decree, as written *"Whatever G-d wants, He does"* (Tehilim 135:6), and *"so shall be My word that goes out from My mouth; it shall not return to Me empty, unless it has done what I desire"* (Isaiah 55:11).

Four: He watches over and directs the lives of all men, He does not abandon any of them (from bestowing good or benefiting them according to their needs - *PL*) nor neglects any of them (from saving them from damages - *PL*). None of their matters, small or great are hidden from Him, and no matter can distract

Him from remembering another matter, as written: *"Why should you say, O Jacob, and speak, O Israel, 'My way has been hidden from the L-ord, and my judgment (i.e. my providence - TL) is passed over from my G-d'?"* (Isaiah 40:27), and *"Do you not know-if you have not heard-an everlasting G-d is the L-ord, the Creator of the ends of the world; He neither tires nor wearies; there is no fathoming His understanding* (i.e. on His providence of all the creations simultaneously - *TL*)" (Isaiah 40:28).

> (*Pas Lechem*: That which the latter verse ascribes the creation specifically to "the ends of the world", this is to convey that G-d's power is infinite, therefore the nature of His handiworks also must be boundless and immeasurable, as in truth they are [physically boundless] among the spiritual creations (souls,etc). However, when G-d's divine wisdom ordained to call into existence a world of finite character, He constrained His power in His handiwork and held it at a certain amount. And this is an amazing feat to the thinking person, and this is what the verse alludes to in saying: "there is no fathoming His understanding")

Five: No created being can benefit or harm either itself or any other creature without the permission of the Creator.

> (*Pas Lechem*: i.e. just like he cannot help himself, so too he cannot help others without the permission of the Creator.)

If a slave has more than one master, and each one has the power to help him, it is not possible for him to put his trust in only one of them, since he hopes to benefit from each master. And if one master can benefit him more than the others, he should trust proportionally more in him, even though he also trusts in the others. And if only one of the masters can benefit him or harm him, certainly he should put his trust only on that master, since he does not hope for benefit from the other masters. Similarly, when a human being will realize that no created being can benefit him or harm him without the permission of the Creator, he will stop being afraid of them or of hoping for anything from them, and he will place his trust in the Creator alone, as written: *"Put not your trust in princes, nor in mortal man who has no help"* (Tehilim 146:3).

(*Pas Lechem*: the expression "nor in mortal man who has no help" alludes to both points simultaneously. (1) That if the generous man helps him, the help is not ascribed to him but rather to the Creator, since he cannot help him without the permission of the Creator. (2) The expression "who has no help" also alludes to that which the generous man also cannot even help himself. Both interpretations are true and simultaneously intended.

Tov Halevanon: That a generous man cannot help due to his own power. Rather the help is from G-d and the man is just an agent, therefore it is more proper to trust in G-d.)

Six: That one is conscious of G-d's abundant goodness to man, and how He brought him into existence out of abundant and pure benevolence and kindness, without man being worthy of this, nor because G-d has any need for him. But rather only out of generosity, benevolence, and goodness, as we explained in the Gate of Examination in this book, and like King David said: *"Many, O L-ord my G-d, are Your wonderful works which You have done, and Your thoughts which are toward us: they cannot be reckoned up in order to You; if I would declare and speak of them, they are more than can be numbered"* (Tehilim 40:5).

(Translator: i.e. how do we know G-d brought man into existence out of pure benevolence and kindness? Because He does not need anything from man. This is logical because man is His creation and a creator does not need anything from His creation. As an illustration (heard from Rabbi Moshe Lazarus), close your eyes and think of a blue-colored orange fruit. You have just created that fruit in your mind. As long as you continue to think about it, it has a form of existence in your mind. Now, do you have any need for that orange? Of course not, it is just the opposite. The orange needs you for everything while you don't need it for anything. So too, we need G-d, not the other way around. His "thoughts" are continuously giving existence to the universe (as brought down in the book Tanya, Shaar Yichud v'Emuna ch. 7: "G-d's Thought and Knowledge of all created beings encompasses each and every creature. For this is its very life-force and that which grants it existence from absolute nothingness."). Therefore, since He has no need for us, granting us existence is a continuous act of pure benevolence and grace. Note that this is just an analogy, not to be taken too literally. For G-d is unknowable to us. Another reason, G-d is infinitely and absolutely perfect in every way. He cannot become any more perfect. Thus, He has no need for anything as explained in Gate 1.)

Seven: That one clearly realizes that all existing things in this world, whether purposeful or accidental have predetermined limits which cannot be increased or decreased from what the Creator has decreed, whether in amount, quality, time, or place. It cannot be numerous if the Creator decreed it few, nor few if the Creator decreed it numerous, nor come late if decreed to come early, nor come early if decreed to come late. And if something appears to be contrary to this, really, it was already pre-decreed with foresight, only that all decrees [are implemented through] causes and means, which in turn have causes and means.

(*Tov Halevanon* commentary: i.e. That incident did not happen by itself, even though this incident is caused by another incident, and the other incident itself is caused by another incident, and so forth until the first cause - all of them came through a decree from G-d. He coordinated all the incidents in a controlled way.

For example: A boat whose crew wanted to go out to sea at this time tomorrow, the Sultan then falsely accused the captain of the ship and delayed him for some time period. During that time period, wars broke out in the sea. When the boat finally set out to sea, the crew feared the wars and wanted to escape through a different route. The boat wound up broken by boulders which were along that route in the sea and the entire crew drowned. The sea then carried a floating case filled with treasures towards the shore. At the same time, the Sultan of a nearby city falsely accused a Tzadik (righteous person) who ran away to the sea shore. At that moment, the case appeared floating near the shore. The righteous man found it and was able to obtain his livelihood from it for the rest of his life.

Behold, this that the first Sultan falsely accused the captain was the beginning of the initial cause of providing for the livelihood of this Tzadik, since if the crew went out to sea earlier, before the wars broke out, they would not have turned towards the dangerous route which broke the ship. The second incident was the breaking out of the wars at that specific time. The third incident, that which the case was able to float on the sea. The fourth incident was that which the sea current pushed the case towards this side of the shore. The fifth, the accusing of the righteous man by the Sultan at that specific time. The sixth incident, that which was put in his heart the idea to run away. The seventh incident, that which he ran away at that specific time and to that specific place.

Behold, all these matters did not happen accidentally, rather, G-d in His wisdom, coordinated that everything happen in its time and place. And even the breaking out of the wars and the drowning of the crew - everything occurred by decrees of G-d, each with its own reason, just that He coordinated in His wisdom to complete all of His will and decrees simultaneously. Strive to understand this because it is deep and this is the author's intent.

... And the final incident (of providing for the tzadik) preceded everything and was the first cause of all the causes which followed (relative to this decree) until this cause of providing for the righteous man materialized. And even so, all the events which preceded this did not occur incidentally, namely, that they did not occur merely for this small first cause which was accomplished. Rather, all these chains of events which accomplished this first cause (of providing for the tzadik), were planned by G-d with foresight, and every incident had its own independent reason and decree. This is something which is beyond our finite minds to grasp, how it is possible that all of these things are coordinated in unison, and each one is not accidental. Rather, everything according to its decree, without one matter contradicting another, and like the verse says: "for the L-ord is a G-d of all-knowledge, and by Him actions are weighed" (Shmuel 2:3).

Likewise, for the development of later causes, for example: When we see a torrent of water which flooded all the inhabitants of a city. It appears that due to the flood a single incident occurred to all those who were in that city. But this is not so, rather, there were other previous causes that occurred with G-d's coordination, so that all those who were decreed to die were assembled together in one place, due to many causes and chains of causes which preceded this cause of flooding, and everything occurring with G-d's foresight.

Translator: note that it was all planned with foresight from the creation of the world as explained in the story of R. Eleazar b. Pedat - Talmud Taanit 25a)

One who does not understand the matters of this world thinks that an immediate cause will force a change in matters, which in turn cause more changes (that present events constantly reshape the future). But really, a single cause is too weak to force a change by itself, as we see one grain of wheat can cause 300 ears of wheat to grow, which each contain 30 grains, so one grain would have produced around ten thousand grains. Can one hide the fact that one grain by itself is incapable of producing this amount? And likewise for other grains that one plants, and likewise we can say for a man or an animal from a drop of seed, or a huge fish from a tiny egg.

(*Lev Tov*: Rather, the true underlying power which causes the seeds to grow into ears of wheat is G-d's original decree from Genesis [that the seemingly biological life process driving the seed would unfold in this way]. And this pre-decree is what drives the matter to actuality through the available means.

Translator: Normally the effect does not exceed the capacities of the cause. Here it is clear that the effect (human being with spiritual soul) is beyond the powers of the cause (physical human seed).)

To busy oneself in trying to bring early what the Creator decreed would come later, or to try to delay what was decreed to come early, or to try to make numerous what was decreed to be few or to try to diminish what was decreed to be numerous in worldly possessions, unless it causes strengthening of G-d's service or accepting His torah (since on religious matters G-d does not decree on a man, rather the free will is in man's own hands, as will be explained - *ML*), - all this is due to (1) weakness in the recognition of G-d's all-knowing understanding (of us and our needs - *PL*), and (2) foolishness in failing to understand the benevolent character of G-d's conducts.

> (*Pas Lechem*: i.e. that all of G-d's conducts with His creations is for their benefit. Through realizing these two points, there will be trust.

> *Translator:* - The Madregos HaAdam wrote that one who worries and tries to earn more than what was decreed for him is like a man inside a moving train pushing the wall to make the train move faster.

The wise man has already hinted this when he said: *"everything has a time and moment under the heaven"* (Koheles 3:1), and afterwards he mentions 28 matters (corresponding to the 28 lunar positions which alludes to astrological fate - *TL*), as he says *"a time to be born, and a time to die.."*, until *"a time for war and a time for peace"*, and also: *"for time and fate will overtake them all"* (Koheles 9:11), and then he said: *"[If you see oppression of the poor, and deprivation of justice and righteousness in the province], wonder not about the matter, for the Highest over the high watches over them, and there are higher ones over them"* (Koheles 5:7). (that really it is not astrological "fate", but rather G-d is guiding everything behind the scenes through chains of causes according to His desire and decrees - *TL*)

> (*Pas Lechem*: If you see oppression of the poor and deprivation of justice, etc., do not wonder, since certainly it has already been decreed on the wicked to get what they deserve, only that G-d will bring their retribution through chains of many causes (which are coordinated with everyone affected). Therefore, their retribution is delayed. But when the causes are finished, they will also be finished. This is

what is meant by *"for the Highest over the high watches over them, and there are higher ones"*, to teach that thus Divine wisdom decided to implement the divine decrees through many causes...

Pas Lechem: (earlier) And if you ask: if it is so that everything was pre-decreed, if so, why does this not happen right away from the beginning, for example, for an almond, why does it start as a bud, then blossoms into a flower, then sprouts a shoot, then a hull, then an almond shell, etc., why didn't ripe almonds grow from the beginning, as we see them now? On this, he answered that this is what Divine wisdom decided - that everything be implemented through chains of many causes and means in a natural looking progression.

Translator's note: the reason G-d made the world in such a way that His decrees are hidden behind "nature" is so that man can have free will to choose between good and evil. Let us consider what would happen if G-d would manifest His presence on the sky in His full power and glory to hit with lightning bolts all those who commit evil deeds. In such a situation virtually all people would start to live in terror and in fear. No man would have the courage to do anything for doing of which would not receive a direct order from G-d. Science and technology would collapse, as no-one would have the courage to research, investigate, or to just speculate - as everyone would be scared that this may act against G-d's intentions. Social life would collapse as no one would utter a word out of terror of saying the wrong thing. Medicine would fall down as doctors would be scared to heal thus breaking G-d's wishes. Most would be too scared to lift a finger for fear of sin and deserving a punishment. People would then live like forced slaves and soon the entire population would die out. In order to avoid such consequences and provide an arena for free will, G-d introduced several prevention measures to His coexistence with people. Hence He almost never openly manifests Himself to living people. He always maintains people in ambiguity about His presence in order to maintain "free will" and the possibility of virtue. Therefore, everything that G-d

does, He does in such a manner that it is ambiguous - i.e.
that it can be explained in many different manners, etc., etc.
(Jan pajak)

Note that this is only one aspect. There's a lot more to it than
that. The primary reason (as heard from Rabbi Mordechai
Kornfeld) is that it has lots in common with raising children
(who is the better parent-the one standing ready with a stick
and carrot, or the one hiding behind the door and letting his
child grow?), coaching independence, and thus becoming
akin to the Creator. The answer lies at the very root of the
need for free will and the requisite amount of it, which is
discussed by the Ramchal in Derech Hash-m (beginning of
ch. 2 of the first section or so) and in Daas Tevunos (where
he offers another, more familiar, explanation).

Related to this point, if G-d would manifest Himself openly to
human beings, it would completely crush their egos. No man
would be capable of thinking highly of himself due to
perceiving just how utterly puny, weak, and insignificant he is
compared to the infinite G-d. This realization would render
him completely and absolutely humble and his divine service
would be forced and meaningless.

Hence, it is necessary for free will that a natural order exists
whose purpose is to provide a misleading appearance that
the world carries itself. Therefore, when nature was created,
with it came the loopholes for interpreting the world
according to the atheistic views. It is essential for G-d's plan
of human free will. For only in such a situation of free will can
a person earn meaningful levels of righteousness and
holiness. This is why the world appears billions of years old
as a result of some cosmological accident, etc. etc. Likewise
G-d created life forms in stages from simple to complex to
make room for a naturalistic explanation, etc. etc. But the
true truth seeker will see the marks of divine wisdom which
are all around us and draw the correct conclusions, as
explained in Gates 1 and 2.

Another reason is as the Ramchal writes (Daas Tevunos
siman 40):

"certainly G-d could have established the world through His omnipotent system, in such a way that everything would be totally incomprehensible to us, not before not after, without cause and effect. If He had done so, no one (atheist) would be able to open their mouths for we would not be able to understand anything whatsoever... but because He wanted us to understand a bit of His ways and attributes - on the contrary He very much wants us to exert ourselves on this..." end quote

Scientific progress has shown so far that the phenomena in the universe is understandable to man. Even the weirdest, most bizarre quantum mechanics, black holes, etc. can nevertheless be fit into human-made mathematical models that we can understand and use to make predictions. Albert Einstein said: "The most incomprehensible thing about the world is that it is comprehensible." This indicates that it is all for man. It is a kind of ladder to come to know a bit of G-d's wisdom and ways at our level.

The ways of judgments of the Creator are too deep, hidden and lofty for us to understand part of them, and all the more so to understand their general principles. And the verse already says: "As the heavens are higher than the earth, so are My ways higher than your ways and My thoughts [higher] than your thoughts" (Isaiah 55:9).

SECOND INTRODUCTION TO BRING COMPLETE TRUST
(2) To know and clearly realize that the Creator is watching him, and neither one's private or public conduct is hidden from Him, nor his innermost being or outer appearance. He also knows whether a man's trust in Him is with a sincere heart or not, as the verse says "G-d knows the thoughts of the heart, that they are vain" (Tehilim 94:11) and "Does not He that tests the heart understand it?" (Mishlei 24:12), and "You alone know the hearts of all men" (Melachim I 8:39).

When this is clearly realized by the one who trusts, it is not proper for him to claim with his lips that he trusts in G-d (in the daily prayers in many places - ML), without trusting in Him in his heart and thoughts, whereby he would be in the category of he of whom the verse says "with their mouths and their lips they honor

Me, but their hearts are far from Me" (Isaiah 29:13).

> (*Pas Lechem*: The reason the author counted this as one of the introductions/prerequisites to trust is only for the phrase: "He also knows whether a man's trust in Him is with a sincere heart or not", that through a man's remembering that G-d observes Him in all of his words and thoughts, he will also remember that included in this is G-d's observing whether or not his trust is sincere.
>
> *Marpe Lenefesh*: When a man realizes that G-d knows the truth, whether what comes out of his lips is the same as what is in his heart, how could he then claim and say that he "truly trusts in G-d", when his heart is not with him. And then G-d will also remove His providence from him as mentioned in the beginning of the introduction to this gate ("..whoever trusts in something other than G-d, the Al-mighty will remove His providence from such a person..."), and then it will be a chillul H-ashem. And it is proper for us to put our eyes and hearts on the things which come out of our lips every day in our prayers, that we claim and say many times that we trust in Him and hope to Him, such as in Pesukei D'Zimra: "Nafshenu Chiksa L'H-ashem", "ki bshem kadsho batachnu", "yehi chasdecha..", and in Ahava Raba: "ki bshem kadshecha hagadol vehanora batachnu", and in the Shmonei Esrei "ve ten sachar tov lchol habotchim b'shimcha b'emes, vsim chelkenu imahem", "ki becha batachnu", and many others. It is proper for every man to put his eye and heart all of his days on the words of this gate, then "lo yevosh v'lo yikalem", not in this world and not in the next.

THIRD INTRODUCTION TO BRING COMPLETE TRUST
(3) That a person trusts in G-d alone for the things he is obligated to trust in (the things that one should not trust in G-d will be explained later), and not to associate Him with anyone else by trusting in Him and one of the created beings because then his trust in G-d will be invalidated in that he associated someone else with G-d. You know what was said about Asa, despite all of his piety, when he relied on the doctors, as written "during his illness, he did not seek help from G-d, but only in the

doctors" (Divrei HaYamim II 16:12) (i.e. he did not also pray), and he was punished for this. And the verse says "Blessed is the man who trusts in the L-ord; the L-ord shall be his refuge" (Yirmiya 17:7).

And it is known that one who entrusts two or more men to do a task, the matter spoils. All the more so, for one who trusts in G-d and man, that his trust in G-d will be ruined (since he equated G-d with a created being, which is a great demeaning of G-d's greatness - *TL*).

> (*Pas Lechem*: The talmud says (Eruvin 50a) "a pot of partners is neither hot nor cold", i.e. that for two people who are entrusted with a task, even though they are of approximately equal worth, nevertheless, each one is not pleased with your trust in him since you also charged the second person to head the task and trusted in him. All the more so that it is hard on G-d to be pleased when you equate a servant with his Master.
>
> Translator: The Rayatz Rebbe would say "bitachon (trust) is when a person finds himself in the middle of the ocean with nothing, not even a piece of straw". i.e. this is how one should view his situation. Heard from D.L.Naiditch)

Furthermore, this will be the strongest factor for denying him the object of his trust, as written "cursed is the man who trusts in men,.. and turns his heart away from G-d" (Yirmiya 17:5).

> (*Marpe Lenefesh*: Rather, let one reflect constantly that G-d is the Cause of all causes, and everyone and everything are merely His agents, as will be explained later on.)

FOURTH INTRODUCTION
That one is very careful and makes a great effort to fulfill what the Creator required of him in His service, to do his mitzvot and to guard oneself from what He has forbidden, just like he seeks that the Creator agrees to do with him in that which he trusts Him, as our sages said "make His will your will so that He will make your will His will, nullify your will to His will so that He will nullify the will of others to your will" (Avot 2:4).

(*Tov Halevanon*: i.e. nullify your taava (physical desires) so that they will not lead you to nullify a commandment of G-d, and separate from what is permitted to you, "so that He will nullify the will of others to your will", i.e. so that His providence on you will be greater than His providence on other people, and everyone in the world will yield for your sake, as the talmud says (Berachos 6b) "the whole world was created for his sake only".)

And the verse says "Trust in the L-ord and do good; so shall you dwell in the land, and verily you shall be fed" (Tehilim 37:3), and "G-d is good to those who hope in Him, to one who seeks Him" (Eicha 3:25).

But, If one trusts in G-d and rebels against Him, how foolish is he, how weak is his intellect and his understanding! For he can see in this world that if an employer appoints a man to do something or refrain from doing something and the man disobeys the instruction, this will be the strongest factor in the employer's refusing to fulfill his side of the deal. All the more so, for one who disobeys the commandments of G-d, for which G-d Himself testified that one who trusts in Him and disobeys Him will have his hopes foiled and his trust will be considered hypocritical.

Rather, he will be like that of who it is written "For what is the hope of the flatterer who deceives, when G-d casts off his soul? Will G-d listen to his cry when trouble comes on him?" (Job 27:8-9), and "Will you steal, murder, commit adultery, swear falsely, offer up to idols, and follow other gods that you know not. And will you come and stand before Me in this house, upon which My Name is called, and say, 'We are saved,' in order to commit all these abominations? Has this house upon which My name is called, become a den of thieves in your eyes? I, too, behold I have seen it, says the L-ord." (Yirmiyahu 7:9-11).

(*Marpe Lenefesh*: Even though G-d has compassion on all His creations, including the wicked, as he explained earlier, even so, for this, one should not think that G-d will forever tolerate him, and trust that G-d will continue bestowing good to him always despite his wickedness. And even though things are going well now, there is no escape from His judgments, and eventually, when He wishes, He will choose a time and place to collect His debt (of justice). Rather it is proper for a man to endeavor to fulfill all of G-d's commandments.

Matanas Chelko: Besides that one must realize that all powers are in G-d's hands, none can prevent Him from doing what He wishes, and further that G-d knows his thoughts, and it is impossible to trick Him. Hence, he cannot claim verbally that he trusts in G-d while he does not really trust Him in his inner being. Thirdly, that he should not associate anything or anyone else with G-d, as before. However, an extra condition is needed, namely, that this is in truth the will of G-d. For, one cannot place his trust in a strong person who can help him unless he knows that the person actually wants to help him. For example, if one tells a poor man: "such and such a person is a very rich man and is able to help you with all your needs. The poor man still should not place his trust in the rich man since he does not know whether the rich man actually wants to help him.

So too, by G-d, there is no doubt that He can perform signs and wonders for a person. But one cannot trust in this unless he knows that G-d truly wants to do so. The one and only way through which a person can know whether G-d wants to help and do for him is only if he himself does the will of G-d. Hence, necessarily, one of the pillars of trust is that he be a righteous person who does the will of G-d. And even though G-d also does the will of the wicked sometimes, nevertheless, they cannot trust in this because they cannot know for sure how long G-d will hold back retribution from them. Unlike the righteous, who can rest assured.
"make His will your will so that He will make your will His will" - the author is telling us that this mishna is the pillar of trust. He who wants to rest assured that G-d will do what he wants, let him do the will of G-d. Otherwise, how can he trust that G-d will do his wish? But if he exerts himself greatly to do the will of G-d, then he can hope and trust that G-d will likewise do his will... (Translator: see Gate 3 Chapter 7 where the

author brings the minimum service whereby a person is assured of receiving continuous divine benefits.)

"Trust in the L-ord and do good; so shall you dwell in the land, and verily you shall be fed" - both things go together. If he wants to trust in G-d, he must do good, as before. And that which the wicked can trust in G-d's trait of kindness and compassion, this is only temporarily. As the Marpe Lenefesh commentary wrote (see above). Hence, the wicked should not trust that G-d's compassion and kindness will continuously bestow on him forever. Rather, he can trust temporarily on G-d's trait of kindness and compassion, that G-d will withhold retribution from him and continue to bestow life to him. But he must repent in the end and he can never know for sure when the time will come that G-d will collect His debt [of justice]. On the other hand, one who does the will of G-d can place his trust in G-d. For through this he is assured that G-d wants to help him and do what's good for him since G-d already promised this.

"Will G-d hear his cry when trouble comes on him?" - hence G-d testified that he does not wish to help and aid a person who transgresses His word. One who thinks to himself that G-d will help him even if he does not fulfill what G-d commanded him to do - this is the greatest folly.

"Has this house upon which My name is called, become a den of thieves in your eyes?" - even though, of all places in the world, the Temple in Jerusalem is the place where prayers are most readily answered and for trusting in G-d, nevertheless, if it has become a den of thieves, already they should no longer trust in this, and they are not assured anymore that if they scream out in prayers that G-d will fulfill their request. (*translator*: for perhaps it is better for them to receive sufferings to atone for their evil deeds than to be saved)

Translator: nevertheless, one must know and trust that his repentance will always be accepted no matter how far he strayed and what he did etc. as the Marpe Lenefesh commentary explained earlier: "Otherwise, he will abandon hope from the favors of G-d, since he is in doubt whether he is worthy of them, and his trust in G-d will diminish. And through this, he will distance from G-d and His torah. Rather, let him reflect that G-d is benevolent to the good and the bad, as written: "His mercy is on all of His creations" (Tehilim 145:9). And through this, he will come closer to G-d and repent and he will become worthy of the good.")

FIFTH INTRODUCTION
A person should realize that every new thing that happens in this world after Genesis is completed in two ways:
First: By G-d's decree and His will that the matter should come into existence.
Secondly: Through intermediate causes and means - some near, some remote, some apparent, some hidden, all of which rush to bring into existence what was decreed, doing so with G-d's help.

(Ramchal: When a matter is decreed, a Bas Kol (Heavenly voice) is proclaimed throughout the mystical worlds which summons and gives the power to the appointed forces needed to carry out the matter.)

An illustration of the causes: Consider the act of drawing up water from the depths of the earth using a wheel system to which buckets are attached and which raises the water from the well. The buckets are the near cause. The remote cause is the man who harnessed an animal to the wheel and compels the animal to move in order to raise the water from the bottom of the well to the surface of the earth.

The intermediate means between the man and the buckets are: the animal, the mechanical contraption of interconnected wheels/gears which turn each other in series, and the rope. If a mishap were to occur to any one of the causes mentioned (i.e. the intermediate means or the near cause - TL), the intended purpose for which they were designed would not be accomplished.

And so it is for other things which come to existence. They cannot be produced by a man or anyone else, but rather, through the decree of G-d, and His preparing all the means through which the thing will be produced, as written *"And by Him, causes are counted"* (Shmuel I 2:3), and *"Who is great in counsel and mighty in carrying it out"* (Yirmiyahu 32:19), and *"it was a cause from G-d"* (Melachim I 12:15). And if the means are blocked, none of the actions which normally bring this matter into existence will succeed.

(*Pas Lechem*: i.e. by Him are all the number of means which cause each and every thing to occur. And if one of the means were missing the thing would not occur. And since it is not so clear from the first verse that He is the First cause which prepares the other causes, one might think that they are merely known to Him in number. Therefore the author brought the second verse "Who is great in counsel and Mighty in carrying it out", which teaches that He is the Master of all causes and the one who carries them out... And if one is still stubborn and wants to say that there is no proof from these two verses. They only teach that the causes are attributed to Him since He is the Creator of everything, therefore the author brought the third verse which teaches that the matter was from G-d with specific intent for that thing.

Matanas Chelko: even for making a loaf of bread, thousands of people are needed such as workers to plant, reap, mill, bake. And each stage requires machines built for sowing, reaping, etc. And the materials are transported through machines on roads and highways, etc. Hence even to make a piece of bread there are thousands of necessary details.. And even though we believe that G-d was behind everything, and that He can do it all without any intermediate means and can create ready to eat bread directly into our home, nevertheless, the author explains, that our eyes can see there is a nature and order that we must recognize and understand. Afterwards, he will explain why G-d wanted things to follow this order.)

When we examine the need for a man to pursue means and exert himself to complete his needs, we can see with our own eyes that for one who needs food and proper food is served before him, nevertheless if he does not exert himself to eat it by lifting the food to his mouth, chewing it, etc., he will not break his hunger. Likewise for someone thirsty, who needs water. And all the more so, if he has no food prepared, until he needs to exert himself through milling flour, kneading, baking, etc . And more so, if he needs to buy the food and prepare it. And even more still, if he has no money to buy them and will need even greater exertion to pursue means to earn the money or to sell the amount he needs from the objects he uses or his other possessions, or the like.

WHY MAN MUST WORK FOR A LIVELIHOOD

There are two reasons why the Creator obligated a man to pursue means and exert himself for his livelihood and other needs.

> (*Tov Halevanon*: Man does not find his food readily like other living creatures which do not need to pursue causes and means.
>
> *Matanas Chelko*: "the Creator obligated a man..." - "hishtadlus" (exertion) is an obligation! It is an obligation to exert oneself to provide for himself and his family. Likewise for all the other things which we are forced to enter into the system of causes and means. It is for two reasons...)

(1) Divine wisdom required the testing of man in the service of G-d or rebellion against Him. Therefore, G-d tests man with what demonstrates his choice in this - needs and lacking for external things such as food, drink, clothing, shelter, and marital relations. G-d commanded man to pursue and attain them through the available means in specific ways (according to the torah - *ML*) and at specific times.

> (*Translator*: G-d knows already what each person will choose. The purpose of testing man is to give him an opportunity to elevate himself in the greatest possible way - by choosing good of his own free will, as explained in Gate 3)

What G-d has decreed that man will attain of them, man will attain fully after the completion of the prepared means.
That which has not been decreed that he will attain - he will not

attain, and the necessary means will be withheld.

Through this process, his free choice of whether he served G-d or rebelled against Him will be demonstrated through his intention and choice, and the man will then deserve either reward or punishment, regardless whether or not he actually achieved his intentions.

> (*Pas Lechem*: the author said "through his intention and choice" because the status of the choice is according to the intention, namely, if he chooses good with bad intentions, such as choosing good with intent for flattery or boasting himself, or arrogance - he is evil. Likewise for the opposite, as our Sages taught us (Nazir 23b) from Yael)

(2) Secondly, if a man were not forced to exert himself in seeking a livelihood, he would kick (become defiant) and chase after sin, and he would ignore his debt of gratitude to G-d for His goodness to him. As written: *"And the harp, and the lyre, the timbrel, and flute, and wine, are in their feasts: but they regard not the work of the L-ord, neither consider the work of His hands"* (Isaiah 5:12), and *"But Yeshurun grew fat, and kicked: you are grown fat, you are grown thick, you are covered with fatness; then he forsook G-d who made him, and lightly esteemed the Rock of his salvation"* (Devarim 32:15). And the sages said *"it is good the study of torah with working for a livelihood because the toil in both removes thoughts of sin, and all torah study without work will in the end be abandoned and bring to sin"* (Avot 2:2). And all the more so for one who has no share in either torah or work, nor directs his attention to any of these pursuits.

> (*Pas Lechem*: From here we see that indulgence in physical pleasures makes a man's heart coarse, thereby causing him to refrain from doing the commandments.
>
> *Tov Halevanon*: If everything were prepared for man, he would be idle to chase after sin. Also his body's nature and physicality would tend to kick and be ungrateful for the favors of G-d due to the delight in his heart, since everything would be ready before him. He would think that he is deserving of all this and he would not realize that it is from G-d.

Marpe Lenefesh: If everything were prepared and ready before a man, he would not have any free choice. And he would remain forever at the same level and he would not deserve any reward or punishment...

Matanas Chelko: In our times, people only want to work a little. Therefore, they lack the necessary exertion and they come to sin. The Creator's intent was that a man work so strenuously from morning until evening that when he returns to his home after a long day of work, he will not have strength to watch television. But, as we said, people do not tire themselves to this extent, so when they return home, they have strength remaining to sin and their evil inclination is still in its full power. The purpose of exertion is to weaken the evil inclination. This is what the sages said "it is good the study of torah with working for a livelihood because the toil in both removes thoughts of sin". In truth, if a man would exert himself in torah to such an extent that his evil inclination would be weakened, then he would have reached the intended purpose and would not need to also exert himself in earning a livelihood. But this path is only for special individuals. The vast majority need to exert themselves in both. Exertion in torah alone is not enough for them. However, the intent for both is the same, namely, that the exertion weakens his strength until he is no longer capable of sinning. Hence, the purpose is not simply to learn torah and work. For if these two do not weaken him to such an extent that he can no longer sin, then he will still come to sin. Rather, the aim is to toil and strain in torah and also in work until both exertions remove thoughts of sin.)

It was out of compassion for man that G-d has compelled him to be occupied with matters of this world and the next for all of his days, and so that he does not seek that which he does not need and which he cannot understand with his limited intellect, such as matters of what was before the creation and of the final end (since these things do not further his perfection and on the contrary - they damage him - PL), as the wise man said *"also the [toil of] the world He has set into their hearts, so that man should not seek the deed which G-d did, from beginning to end."*

(Koheles 3:11).

WHEN G-D REMOVES THE BURDEN OF EARNING A LIVELIHOOD FROM A MAN

If a man strengthens himself in the service of G-d, resolves to fear Him, trusts in Him for his religious and secular matters, steers away from reprehensible things (such as anger or arrogance - *PL*), strives for the good midot (character traits), does not rebel in prosperity nor turn towards leisure, is not enticed by the evil inclination, nor seduced by the witchery of this world - the burden of exerting himself in the means to a livelihood will be removed from him, since the two reasons mentioned above no longer apply to him. Namely, to test him on his choice and to protect him from rebelling during prosperity. His livelihood will come to him without strain (of the heart - *PL*) or toil (of the limbs - *PL*), according to his needs, as written *"G-d will not bring hunger to the righteous"* (Mishlei 10:3).

(*Tov Halevanon*: "the witchery of this world" refers to the worldly pleasures which spellbind the eyes of the one who gazes at them until he thinks they are good for him but he does not realize their ultimate end.

Pas Lechem: *"removes the burden.."* - since he no longer needs to be tested because his heart has already strengthened in the service of G-d, and he is full of fear and trust of Him, and also he is not liable to rebel, so why should G-d trouble him further?

Matanas Chelko: This is another great principle. If a man thinks for whatever reason that he no longer needs to engage in the pursuit of a livelihood. This is only justified if he is clinging to G-d. Not because he merely trusts in G-d. Many people mistakenly think that the amount of hishtadlus (exertion for livelihood) is proportional to the amount of trust a person has. This is not correct. A man can have great trust but if he has not yet reached the level that he is straining himself as before or it is still necessary to test him whether or not he will do only the will of G-d, then even if he has much tranquility, he is still under obligation to exert himself in his livelihood....[see there at length]...In our times, if one learns in yeshiva or Kollel and has some sort of plan on how to support himself and his family - this is considered Torah study with work. For that which the sages said that one must combine torah and work, their intent was not that every person must specifically work but rather that he has some sort of plan... nevertheless he is lacking the second reason, namely, that one must strain himself until he has no strength left to come to sin. Therefore, he is under duty to strain himself in torah study to this extent.)

If one asks: Behold we see some tzadikim (very righteous people) which do not receive their livelihood except after hard and strenuous toil, while many transgressors are at ease, living a good, pleasant life?
We will say: The prophets and the chasidim (extremely pious) already investigated this matter. One of them said *"[Righteous are you, O L-rd, when I plead with You: yet let me talk with You of your judgments:] Why does the way of the wicked prosper? why are all they happy that deal very treacherously?"* (Yirmiyahu 12:1), and another *"Why do You show me iniquity and look upon mischief; and plunder and violence are before me; and the one who bears quarrel and strife endures?"* (Chavakuk 1:3), and *"for a wicked man surrounds the righteous; therefore, justice emerges perverted"* (Chavakuk 1:4), and *"Why should You be silent when a wicked man swallows up one more righteous than he?"* (Chavakuk 1:13), and another one said *"Behold these are wicked, yet they are tranquil in the world and have increased wealth."* (Tehilim 73:12), and *"But for naught I cleansed my heart and bathed my hands with cleanliness"* (Tehilim 73:13), and another said *"And now we praise the bold transgressors, those who work wickedness are built up, they tempt G-d, and they have, nevertheless, escaped."* (Malachi 3:15), and many more like this.

But the prophet refrained from giving an answer because each specific case has its own particular reason (there is no general answer which includes everything - *TL*). Therefore Moshe Rabeinu commented on this in the torah saying: *"the hidden things belong to G-d"* (Devarim 29:28), and the wise man said in connection to this *"If you see the oppression of the poor, and perverting of justice and righteousness in a province, marvel not at the matter"* (Koheles 5:7), and the verse says: *"the Rock, His deeds are perfect for all His ways are justice"* (Devarim 32:4).

(i.e. ultimately, the matter is hidden and concealed by its nature and is beyond the powers of the human mind to grasp - *PL*)

WHY THE RIGHTEOUS SOMETIMES SUFFER

Nevertheless, I saw fitting to attempt to clarify this matter that should be to some extent satisfactory (so that it won't be so difficult - *TL*).

The possible reasons why a tzadik is prevented from obtaining his livelihood without effort and must instead exert himself for it and be tested by it is as follows.

1. A previous sin for which it is necessary to pay him for it, as written *"the tzadik will pay in the land"* (Mishlei 11:31).

> (*Marpe Lenefesh*: As the sages said (Kidushin 39b): "He whose merits outweighs his sins is punished (Rashi: in this world to cleanse him from his sins, so that he receives complete reward in the World to Come) and is as though he had burnt the whole Torah, not leaving even a single letter; while he whose sins outweighs his merits is rewarded (Rashi: to pay him the reward for his merits in this world so as to banish him in the World to Come) and is as though he had fulfilled the whole Torah, not omitting even a single letter!"
>
> *Translator*: and since the wicked man is unable to receive the reward of Olam Haba due to corrupting his soul too much, so might as well give him some good here - *Lev Eliyahu*.)

2. In the way of exchanging, to pay him more good in Olam Haba (the afterlife), as written *"to benefit you in your end"* (Devarim 8:16)

> (*Marpe Lenefesh*: These are "Yisurim shel Ahava" (chastening of love) which are not due to sins, as the talmud says (Berachos 5a): "if he examined his deeds and did not find any sins let him be sure that these are Yisurim shel

Ahava, as written (Mishlei 3:12): 'For whom G-d loves He chastens'", i.e. to increase his reward in Olam Haba more than his merits.

Pas Lechem: To exchange for him a fleeting world for an eternal world.)

3. To demonstrate his good bearing and good acceptance of suffering in the service of G-d, so that others will learn from him, as you know from the matter of [the book of] Job.

(*Marpe Lenefesh*: That he receives everything with a good countenance, and he does not rebel in sufferings so that others will learn from him and see him and notice him and desire to serve G-d even though they don't have all their lusts, and even though they are in poverty, hardship or in painful sicknesses as we find with Job and many other sages, who were in suffering yet did not stop from torah and service, and as is known of Hillel who was extremely poor, and others who needed to labor for their livelihoods and nevertheless studied the torah.

Alternative explanation:

Pas Lechem: To show the world that the Tzadik bears the bad of this world, with good patience and a good countenance, and despite his suffering, he does not budge away from the service of his Creator in order to ease the bad. Unlike the wicked, that even for something he is forced to bear, he bears it with an angry heart, and therefore he throws off the yoke of service in order to ease his troubles.

Tov Halevanon: He bears his sufferings and is not begrudging towards G-d and accepts them with a good countenance)

4. Due to the wickedness of his generation, G-d tests him with poverty, hardship, or sickness to demonstrate/contrast his piety and service of G-d unlike them, as written *"Indeed, he bore our illnesses, and our pains he carried them"* (Isaiah 53:4).

(*Pas Lechem*: Here G-d knows that the people of his generation won't learn from him and they will get no benefit from this. Nevertheless, G-d tests him in order to demonstrate his level and worth and contrast it with them.

That even though they are in enjoyment and he is in a life of suffering, they are ungrateful towards G-d while he is good with Him and serves Him in truth and wholeheartedly. The intent in this is so that they will acknowledge G-d's justice in the end of days when they will see the exceedingly great reward of the Tzadik. And like our sages said in Pirkei Avot 5:3, "Avraham was tested with ten trials..to show his high esteem."

Marpe Lenefesh: Due to the wickedness of the generation, sometimes G-d sends suffering to a Tzadik to atone for the sins of the generation (to avert disasters or the like), and without a doubt, his reward will not be withheld and the wicked will be paid what they deserve, as Rashi explained on the verse he cited)

5. Due to his not being sufficiently zealous in standing up for G-d, and exacting justice (i.e. protesting - *TL*) from men of his generation, as you know from the story of Eli and his sons, as the verse says *"And it will be that everyone who is left in your house, will come to prostrate himself before him for a silver piece and a morsel of bread"* (Shmuel 2:36).

(*Pas Lechem*: As the Talmud says (Shabbat 54b): "Whoever can forbid his household [to commit a sin] but does not, is seized (held accountable) for [the sins of] his household; [if he can forbid] the men of his city, he is seized for [the sins of] the men of his city; if the whole world, he is seized for [the sins of] the whole world")

Translator: There is another general purpose to suffering for everyone including children as explained in Gate 2 ch.5. Here is an excerpt:
Later on he is subjected to illnesses and meets with painful incidents so that he recognizes the world, and that its nature is not concealed from him. Thus he is put on his guard against trusting in this world thereby permitting his lusts to rule over him, in which case he would become like the animals that neither think nor understand; as it is written *"Be ye not as the horse or as the mule which have no understanding"* (Tehilim 32:9).

Tov Halevanon: *"illnesses"* - such as chicken pox and measles. *"painful incidents"* - many weaknesses come in the boyhood years. PL - accidents such as stepping on a metal nail.

"Be ye not as the horse or as the mule" - they need to be leashed and muzzled, so too man. The painful incidents humble his lusts.

"so that he recognizes the world" - how a person's situation can change swiftly from contentment to pain so that he realizes not to trust in it and its tranquility - rather to always be afraid and to seek refuge in G-d's shadow.

Marpe Lenefesh: If a human being had only constant good in this world, he would forget and not recall the matters of his final end, and he would trust (hope) in this world and follow the musings of his heart and his lusts for all of his days. Therefore, it was among the divine plan to send him sometimes bad illnesses, even during his youth in order that he recognize and know that there is no complete good in this world. And even if he is currently in a very good situation, the bad illnesses can come and ruin his joy, so that he won't trust in this world.

End Quote.

Another reason for suffering explained by the kabalists is to rectify something done in past lives. Most people are said to have lived previously in past lives (see shaar gilgulim). So for example, someone born into a life of misery and suffering for no apparent reason whatsoever - this may be in order to rectify something from a past life. For example, the Zohar states that the Jewish slaves in Egypt who born and died doing hard labor slavery work for Pharaoh were reincarnations of the generation of the builders of the Tower of Bavel.)

WHY THE WICKED SOMETIMES PROSPER

Sometimes G-d sends good to the wicked for the following reasons:

1. A previous good deed he did, to pay him in this world, as written *"And He repays those He hates to their face, to destroy them"* (Devarim 7:10) which Onkelos renders: "He pays those He

hates for their good deeds during their lives to destroy them".

2. As a temporary deposit, until G-d gives him a righteous son who is worthy of it, as written *"he prepares but the tzadik (righteous) will wear it"* (Job 27:17), and *"to the sinner He has given a preoccupation to gather and to accumulate, to give to him who is good in G-d's sight"* (Koheles 2:26).

3. Sometimes the money is the chief cause of his evil (in the next world) or death (in this world), as written *"There is a grievous evil that I saw under the sun; riches kept by their owner for his harm"* (Koheles 5:12) (such as Korach or Naval - *PL*).

4. Sometimes it is to give him time to repent and become worthy of it, as you know of the story of Menashe.

5. His father did good and it is fitting to benefit him in the merit of his father, as said to Yehu ben Nimshi *"four generations of your descendants will sit on the throne of Israel"* (Melachim II 10:30), and *"He who walks innocently is righteous; fortunate are his sons after him"* (Mishlei 20:7), and *"I was young, and have aged, and I have not seen a righteous man forsaken nor his descendants begging bread"* (Tehilim 37:25).

6. Sometimes it is to test those who are deceptive or have an evil interior. When they see the wicked prosper, they quickly stray from the service of G-d and hasten to win the favor of the wicked and to learn from their actions. In this way it will be clarified the pure men to G-d and it will be demonstrated who was faithful to G-d in bearing at a time when the wicked rule and persecute him. He will receive reward from the Creator for this, as you know of the story of Eliyahu and Isabel or Yirmiyahu and the kings of his generation.

> (*Pas Lechem*: The intended purpose of all this was so that the pure men "will receive reward from the Creator for this".
>
> *Marpe Lenefesh*: Through this it will be demonstrated who was of good, pure heart to G-d and faithful in His service. And even though the wicked were ruling over him and

humiliating him, he bears everything and knows that their success is temporary and eventually G-d will collect His debt. And he doesn't learn from their ways and will receive reward for this. But if G-d were to punish the wicked immediately, and reward the righteous right away, there would be no room for free will (which was the purpose of creation), and everyone would hasten to do good and receive reward quickly and everyone would fear swift punishment.

CHOICE OF OCCUPATION:
Since it has been clarified the obligation for a man to pursue the means for a livelihood, now we will clarify that not every man is required to pursue every possible means.

The possible means are numerous. Some occupations are easy, requiring little strain such as shop keeping or light work with the hands such as sewing, writing, contracting businesses, hiring sharecroppers or workers, supervisors.

Some occupations require hard physical labor such as tanning, mining iron or copper, smelting metals, heavy transport, constant travel to faraway places, working and plowing land, or the like,

For one who is physically strong and intellectually weak, it is fitting to choose an occupation among those that require physical exertion according to what he can bear.
He who is physically weak but intellectually strong should not seek among those which tire the body but should instead tend towards those who are light on the body and that he will be able to sustain .

Every man has a preference for a particular work or business over others. G-d has already implanted in his nature a love and fondness for it, as He implanted in a cat's nature the hunting of mice, or the falcon to hunt smaller birds, the deer to trap snakes. Some birds hunt only fish, and likewise, each animal species has a liking and desire for particular plants or animals, which G-d has implanted to be the means for its sustenance, and the structure of its body and limbs is suited for that thing. The long bill and legs of a fish catching bird, or the strong teeth and claws of the lion, horns of the ox and ram (i.e. for defense - *TL*), while animals whose sustenance is from plants do not have the tools to hunt and kill.

Similarly you will find among human beings character traits and body structures suited for certain businesses or activity. One who finds his nature and personality attracted to a certain occupation, and his body is suited for it, that he will be able to bear its demands - he should pursue it, and make it his means of earning a livelihood, and he should bear its pleasures and pains, and not be upset when sometimes his income is withheld. Rather let him trust in G-d that He will support him all of his days.

> (*Pas Lechem*: For example, one for who the trait of compassion dominates him should distance from becoming a butcher. And likewise, the sages said: "a kapdan (irritable person) should not be a teacher" (Pirkei Avot 2:5), and similarly for other traits.)

INTENTIONS WHEN WORKING FOR A LIVELIHOOD
And he should have intention when his mind and body is occupied with one of the means of earning a living to fulfill the commandment of the Creator to pursue the means of the world, such as working the land, plowing and sowing it, as written: *"And G-d took the man and placed him in Gan Eden to work it and to guard it"* (Bereishit 2:15), and also to use other living creatures for his benefit and sustenance, and for building cities and preparing food, and to marry a woman and have relations to populate the world.

He will be rewarded for his intentions in heart and mind to serve G-d whether or not his desire is accomplished, as written: *"If you eat from the toil of your hands, you are praiseworthy, and it is good for you"* (Tehilim 128:2), and our sages of blessed memory said: *"Let all your actions be for the sake of Heaven (to serve G-d)"* (Avot 2:12).

In this way, his trust in G-d will be intact, undamaged by the toiling in the means to earn a livelihood, as long as his intention in heart and mind is for the sake of Heaven (to do the will of G-d that the world be populated and built up).

> (*Tov Halevanon*: It will not damage that which he is made idle from torah study and service of G-d since this too will be considered for him as righteousness and service.)

One should not think that his livelihood depends on particular means and that if these means fail, his livelihood will not come from a different means. Rather, trust in the Al-mighty, and know that all means are equal for Him. He can provide using whatever means and at any time and however He so wishes, as written: *"for with the L-ord there is no limitation to save with many or with few"* (Shmuel I 14:6), and *"But you must remember the L-ord your G-d, for it is He that gives you strength to make wealth, in order to establish His covenant which He swore to your forefathers, as it is this day."* (Devarim 8:18), and *"Not by might nor by power, but by My spirit, says the L-ord of Hosts"* (Zecharia 4:6).

*** Chapter 4 ***
- When trust applies and when it does not

The concerns for which the believer is obligated to put his trust in G-d are of two categories. (1) matters of this world, and (2), matters of Olam Haba (afterlife). Matters of this world subdivide to two divisions.

(1) matters of this world for the benefit of this world. (2) matters of this world for the benefit of Olam Haba (the afterlife).

The matters of this world for the benefit of this world subdivide to three parts:
(1) what is beneficial for the body only.
(2) what contributes to one's maintenance or enables one to gain wealth and various possessions.
(3) what is beneficial for [dealing with] one's household, wife and relatives, one's friends and enemies, and for those above and below him among the various classes of people.

Matters of this world for the benefit Olam Haba subdivide to two parts.
(1) Duties of the heart and limbs which relate to oneself only, and whose actions do not result in benefit or damage to others.
(2) Duties of the limbs which cannot be done without association with another person, where one of them is active and the other is passive. For example, giving charity, acts of kindness, teaching of wisdom, instructing others to do good or to refrain from evil.

Matters of the afterlife subdivide to two parts.
(1) The reward that is deserved.
(2) That which is a special kindness which the Creator bestows to the pious and to the prophets in Olam Haba.

THE 7 CATEGORIES TO TRUST IN
Thus all things for which one trusts in the Creator fall into 7 categories:
(1) matters of the body alone.
(2) matters of one's possessions and means of earning a livelihood.

(3) matters of one's wife, children, relatives, friends, and enemies [and for those above and below him].

(4) duties of the heart and limbs which only benefit or damage oneself.

(5) duties of the limbs which affect others as well, whether benefiting or harming.

(6) reward in the afterlife according to one's conduct in this world.

(7) reward in the afterlife from the Creator in the way of kindness on His treasured ones and those who love Him (i.e. to increase their reward due to their love and clinging to G-d - TL), as written: *"How great is Your goodness that You have hidden away for those who fear You; You have done for those who trust in You before the sons of men!"* (Tehilim 31:20)

Since I have explained the fundamental introductions (in chapter 3) which make it possible for one to place his trust in the Al-mighty, it is proper for me to follow them with an explanation of the proper way of trust in each of the seven categories, through which one should trust in G-d and in something besides Him.

(*Tov Halevanon*: i.e. To explain which is the proper way of trust, that can be called complete/flawless trust in G-d versus the trust which is mixed with trusting in something besides G-d such as one who trusts in G-d and also in some means, which would not be a proper and just trust.

Marpe Lenefesh: Namely, if he regards them as means between himself and G-d, and that they are merely agents from G-d as will be explained)

FIRST CATEGORY - MATTERS OF THE BODY ALONE

For the first category, matters of the body alone, these are: his life and death, his income for obtaining food, clothing and shelter, his health and illness, his traits. The proper way of trust in the A-lmighty for all of these matters is to submit oneself to the course the Creator has decreed for him in these matters, and to place one's trust in G-d and to know that none of these matters can come to be unless it was previously determined by G-d that this would be the most proper situation for his matter in this world and in Olam Haba (the afterlife), and ultimately the greatest good for him (even if right now it appears to his eye to be not good, certainly, it is the best thing for him for his ultimate end - *PL*), and that the Creator has exclusive, total control over all of these matters. In none of them can any created being advise any plan, or exercise any control except through His permission, decree, and judgment.

> (*Pas Lechem*: (on the 3 terms: **permission, decree, judgment**) To not think that some human being's advice can possibly be beneficial unless it is through the permission and decree of the Creator. For example, regarding the healing of a sick person, the talmud expounds [on the verse Ex. 21:19]: "from this we learn that **permission** has been given to the physician to heal". The power in nature to heal through medicinal means is a permission of the Creator. This is a universal matter. And this is combined with the **decree** of G-d who decreed that this illness be healed through this specific doctor, as the talmud says (Avoda Zara 58a) "through such and such a doctor, using such and such a medicine". This is for the good category. On the bad category, if a man planned to harm him and succeeded, or that he led him in the bad path, and caused him to stumble, certainly, this **judgment** was sentenced by G-d, otherwise, he would not have succeeded.
>
> *Matanas Chelko*: For all matters of this world, such as the things relevant to his body, home, or livelihood - everything was already pre-decreed by the Creator, and no man has any power or authority on these matters. This is one of the foundations of trust - that no man has any power in this. Therefore, there is no need to fear other people for none of them can benefit or harm him in any way.

And just like one's life and death, health and sickness, are not in the hands of others, so too, one's livelihood, clothing and other bodily needs are also not in their control.

With clear faith that his matters are given over to the decrees of the Creator, and that the Creator's choice for him is the best choice, it is also his duty to be engaged in means which appear to be beneficial to him and to choose what seems to be the best choice under the circumstances, and the Al-mighty will do according to what He has already pre-decreed.

> (*Pas Lechem*: The author specifically stated the passive form of the verb "to be engaged" (in means...) instead of the active form "to engage" (in means...) since we are talking about a person who fully believes that all his movements are given over to the hands of the Creator, and if he does some thing, he is not doing it. Rather it is being done to him by G-d, like an ax in the hands of a woodchopper.
>
> Translator: In Gate 3 chapter 8 the author explains this in more details and notes that it is beyond the ability of human understanding to grasp. see there with the commentaries essential reading.)

An example of this: Even though a human being's end and number of days are determined by the Creator's decree, nevertheless, it is a man's duty to pursue means to survive such as food and drink, clothing, and shelter according to his needs, and he must not leave this to the Al-mighty, and think: "if the Creator has pre-decreed that I will live, then my body will survive without food all the days of my life. Therefore, I will not trouble myself in seeking a livelihood and toiling in it".

Likewise, one should not put himself in danger while trusting on the decree of the Creator [that he will live a set time], drinking poisonous drink or going to battle lions or other dangerous animals without necessity, or to cast himself into the sea or into fire, or other similar things that a man is not sure of them and puts his life in danger. And the verse has already warned us in saying *"You shall not try the L-ord, your G-d"* (Devarim 6:16), because either one of two things will happen.

> (*Matanas Chelko*: "to battle lions or other dangerous animals without necessity" - the [extra] words "without necessity" come to hint that if one was attacked by a lion, he should not give up hope and think he has no chance of being saved. Rather, he should trust in G-d to save him, similar to what

| David did (Samuel 17:36-37).

Either he will die, and it will be considered as if he killed himself, and he will be held accountable for this just as if he had killed another man, despite that his death in this fashion was a decree of the Al-mighty and occurred with His permission.

> (*Tov Halevanon*: i.e. even though this person died through putting himself in danger and it was already predecreed by G-d that he would die through this danger and at that time. Nevertheless, he will be punished like one who murders another person, despite that the other person's death was predecreed. Even so, the murderer is guilty [since he had free will, and the decree of death could have been fulfilled through another way - Translator].)

And we have already been commanded not to murder another human being in any form from the verse: *"do not murder"* (Shmot 20:13). And the closer the murdered is to the murderer, the more the punishment should be severe, as written: *"on pursuing his brother with a sword, corrupting his mercy"* (Amos 1:11). And similarly the punishment for one who kills himself will undoubtedly be very great.

This is like a slave whose master commanded him to guard a place for a fixed time, and warned him not to leave the place until his messenger will come. When the slave saw that the messenger was late in coming, he abandoned his post, and the master became furious at him and punished him severely. Similarly, one who causes his own death (by doing dangerous things) moves out of the service of G-d and into rebellion against Him, by putting himself in mortal danger.

This is why you will find Shmuel say (to G-d): *And Shmuel said, 'How shall I go? For, if Saul hears, he will kill me.' And the L-ord said, "You shall take a heifer with you, and you shall say, 'I have come to slaughter (a sacrifice) to the L-ord.'"* (Shmuel I 16:2).

And this was not considered a lack of trust in the Al-mighty, and the answer from G-d to him shows that his zeal in this was appropriate (since G-d does not do public miracles without great necessity - *TL*), and G-d answered him: *"You shall take a heifer with you, and you shall say, 'I have come to bring an offering to the L-ord.'"* (Shmuel I 16:2). If this were considered a lack of trust G-d would have answered him: *"I cause death and grant life. I strike, and I heal"* (Devarim 32:39), or something similar, as He answered Moshe when Moshe claimed: *"But I am slow of speech and slow of tongue"* (Shmot 4:10), answering him *"Who has made a man's mouth? Who makes a man mute or deaf, seeing or blind"* (Shmot 4:11). And if Shmuel, with his perfect righteousness did not find it a light matter to put himself to a slight risk of danger, and even though he would be doing so by the command of G-d, as He commanded him *"Fill your horn with oil, and go, I shall send you to Yishai, the Bethlehemite, for I have seen for Myself a king among his sons"* (Shmuel I 16:1), all the more so for someone not commanded by G-d, that this would be considered reprehensible.

> (*Pas Lechem*: If you ask: "why was it considered a lacking by Moshe but not by Shmuel?". The answer is that Moshe was commanded "go and speak...", therefore certainly he will be granted the power of speech and he will be able to speak. Therefore [G-d rebuked him]: "Who has made a man's mouth?.." However, by Shmuel, his question was not against the command. It was possible for him to fulfill the command to anoint David and afterwards for Saul to kill him.)

(The second possibility) is that he will be saved by G-d's help. Then his merits will be annulled and he will lose his reward, as our sages said on this matter (Shabbat 32a): *"a man should never put himself in danger thinking that a miracle will be performed for him, because maybe no miracle will be done for him, and even if a miracle is done for him, his merits are reduced"*. And Yaakov our forefather said *"I am not worthy from all Your kindnesses"* (Bereishit 32:11), to which the Targum explains: *"my merits have diminished due to all of Your favors and kindnesses."*

PROPER TRUST IN MATTERS OF EARNING A LIVELIHOOD

What we have explained for matters of life and death, also

applies to the duty to pursue means for health, food, clothing, shelter, good habits and distancing from their opposite - (he should engage in them) while firmly believing that the means to these things do not help at all in attaining them, without the decree of the Creator. Then, when a farmer must plow his field, clear it from weeds, sow it, and water it when rainwater is not available, let him trust in the Creator to make it fertile, and to protect it from plagues, to increase and to bless the crops. And it is not proper to leave the land unworked and unsowed and to trust G-d and rely on His decree that it will grow fruit without being sown first.

> *Matanas Chelko*: This is a powerful illustration from farmers.. For everyone can see that the farmer cannot claim it was all his own making. For even after all the work of plowing, sowing, etc., he must still rely on G-d for rain, and that the rain be not too much and not too little. This is a tremendous illustration on the ways of faith from which one can apply to all matters.
>
> *Translator*: Another illustration: The Jews in the Sinai desert received manna daily for 40 years. Based on a person's spiritual level, the manna would arrive daily either far away in the desert or directly at his doorstep. Thus even though the person was forced to exert himself to search in the desert, nevertheless, he knew that the portion he eventually found as well as the amount of exertion he had to do was pre-decreed for him from the beginning. So too, a person must exert himself according to what he needs. But at the same time, he must realize that the amount he eventually earns was designated for him by G-d from the beginning and that his exertion did not increase or decrease this amount.)

And likewise workers, merchants, and contractors are under a duty to pursue their livelihood while trusting in G-d that their livelihood is in His hands and under His control, that He guarantees to provide a man (as the verse "who gives sustenance to all flesh" - *PL*) and fully provides for him through whatever means He wishes. One should not think that the means can benefit or harm him in the least.

If one's livelihood comes through one of the means he worked on, it is proper for him not to trust in this source, rejoice in it, intensify in it, and turn his heart to it. For this will weaken his trust in the Al-mighty. It is improper to think that this source will be more beneficial to him than what was pre-decreed from the Creator. He should not rejoice for having pursued and engaged in it. Rather, he should thank the Creator who provided for him after his labor, and that He did not make his work and struggle result in nothing, as written: *"If you eat the toil of your hands, you are praiseworthy, and it is good for you"* (Tehilim 128:2).

> (*Matanas Chelko*: hence, the labor and the livelihood are two unconnected things. The labor is a kind of tax payment, and if through this he receives his livelihood and eats, he is also under duty to thank G-d for the food.
>
> *Translator*. I once asked a taxi driver in Israel if he makes good money driving. He corrected me saying "the taxi driving is my tikun (rectification), and the money is from G-d. The two are not connected. They're separate things.")

A pious man once said: "I am amazed of he who gives to another what the Creator decreed for the latter, and afterwards reminds the latter of the favor he did for him, and seeks to be thanked for this. And I am even more amazed by one who receives his livelihood from another who is forced to provide for him and then submits himself before him, pleases him and praises him."

> (*Marpe Lenefesh*: i.e. the recipient does not give praise and thanks to G-d who provided his livelihood through the donor, and appointed the donor as a caretaker of him. Rather, he submits only to the donor and flatters him as if the donor provided him of his own...and likewise he wrote later on "if only they realized that no human being has the power to give or prevent anything except to he who the Creator decreed - they would not hope to anyone other than Him, etc". And he wrote this again several times. This seems to be a contradiction (since the donor had free will whether or not to give to him). The answer to this is that the completion of something is not in man's hands. Rather, only the free will

and resolve to do it [is in man's hands], and G-d is the one who brings all things to completion...

Therefore this is the explanation here - a man is under duty to choose and resolve to separate from his money according to his generosity in order to give charity to the poor or to this poor man. And when the Creator desires to provide for this poor man through this donor, he arranges that they meet in one place so that this donor will give to this poor man, or sometimes to another according to His wisdom. Or if the man is not good before Him, G-d will make him stumble with bad people or other mishaps. But the main thing is that one tries to do the duty that is placed on him - to give charity and to do kindness. And if he is prevented, then he did his part and will receive full reward from G-d. Likewise for all mitzvot and all acts in the world as he will explain later on... And with this you will understand what he wrote earlier in the beginning of chapter 3: "and all mercy and compassion that a man is shown from anyone besides G-d is really derived from G-d's mercy and compassion", see there. That G-d puts in the heart of this one to give to that one. With this introduction many difficult things are clear in the details of G-d's guidance of His world and through this you will understand most of this gate, with G-d's help.

Rabbi Yaakov Emden: Nevertheless, it is certainly a duty to thank and praise one's benefactor and not to think that one is exempt since the good came from G-d.... (see there in Masoret Yisrael edition for more)

Matanas Chelko: the recipient should not feel inferior and less thereby submitting himself towards the rich man and speak to him like a poor man...)

If one's livelihood fails to come through the means he has worked on, it is possible that the money allocated to him for the day has already reached his hands (and that he doesn't realize it - *PL*) or that it will come through other means.

However the case, it is proper for him to engage in the means of earning a livelihood and not to be lax in pursuing after them, provided they are suited to his traits and physical abilities, as I previously explained. And all the while, he should trust in G-d, that He will not abandon him (in providing his needs - *PL*), neglect him (regarding his physical health - *PL*), or ignore him (in whatever trouble befalls him - *PL*) as written *"The L-ord is good, a stronghold on a day of trouble and knows (Rashi - the needs of) those who trust in Him"* (Nachum 1:7)

> (*Pas Lechem*: The first half of the verse teaches that G-d does not ignore his troubles while the second half includes the other two matters, that G-d does not abandon him nor neglect him)

PROPER TRUST IN MATTERS OF HEALTH AND SICKNESS

Similarly, we will say regarding health and sickness. A man is placed under a duty to trust in the Creator in this, while working on maintaining his health according to the means whose nature promotes this, and to fight sickness according to the customary ways, as the Creator commanded *"and he shall surely heal him"* (Shemot 21:19). All of this, without trusting in the means of health or illness that they could help or hurt without the permission of the Creator.

And when one puts his trust in the Creator, He will heal him with or without a means, as written: *"He sends His word and heals them"* (Tehilim 107:20).

> (*Pas Lechem*: From this verse we see that it is really His word, namely, His decree that heals - not the means.
>
> Translator: Rabbi Avigdor Miller would say that in ancient times bloodletting was a popular medical procedure. Today it is neither accepted nor effective. This does not mean that it was not effective back then. Actually it was. The science of the times had logical reasons why it should work, and people believed in those reasons. Therefore G-d healed them through the bloodletting. So too today, medical technology makes us believe certain medicines and medical procedures should work, and therefore G-d heals us through those.)

It is even possible that He will heal him through something that is normally very harmful, as you know from the story of Elisha and the bad water, that he healed their damaging properties with salt (Melachim II 2:19), and similarly *"And G-d showed him a tree and he tossed it into the waters [and the waters became sweet]"* (Shemot 15:25), And the Midrash Tanchuma there explains that this was a bitter, oleander tree. Another example, *"let him smear crushed figs on the boils, and he will heal"* (Isaiah 38:21) (and figs normally damage even healthy flesh - *PL*). And you already know of what happened to the pious king Asa when he trusted in the doctors, and removed his trust in G-d regarding his illness, the sharp rebuke he received for this (i.e. because he did not pray to be healed). And the verse says: *"For He brings pain and binds it; He wounds, and His hands heal."* (Job 5:18).

SECOND CATEGORY - POSSESSIONS AND MEANS OF EARNING A LIVELIHOOD

(Previously he spoke on trusting in the livelihood itself, that certainly it will come through whatever means employed. Now he will speak on proper trust when engaging in the means themselves. understand this. - *PL*)

For the second category, the matters of man's possessions, means of financial gain in his various pursuits, whether in commerce, skilled trades, peddling, business management, official appointments, property rentals, banking, work of kings, treasurers, contracting, writing work, other types of work, going to faraway deserts and seas, and other similar things, from what people toil in to amass money, and increase the superfluous. The proper way of trust in the Al-mighty for this is to engage in the means which G-d has made available to him to the extent necessary for his maintenance and sufficient for his needs of this world (i.e. his minimum necessary needs only - *TL*).

And if the Creator will decree for him more than this, it will come to him without trouble or exertion, provided he trusts in the Al-mighty for it and does not excessively pursue the means nor inwardly trust in them in his heart.

And if the Creator has not decreed for him more than his sustenance, even if all those in heaven and earth were to try to increase it, they would not be capable by any way nor by any means. And when one trusts in G-d, he will find peace of mind and tranquility of spirit, confident that G-d will not give over his portion to someone else, nor send it to him earlier or later than the time He decreed for it.

(*Pas Lechem*: A man's nature is to desire to indulge a bit in luxuries beyond his subsistence needs. Only that, he should not squander his time in occupying himself in this, since it is not essential. Rather, let one trust in G-d that he will find his desire also in this [i.e. in living at subsistence level], because "G-d will fulfill the desire of them that fear Him" Tehilim 119:15)

PROPER TRUST FOR THE WEALTHY

Sometimes the Creator directs the livelihood of many men through one man. This is in order to test that man whether he will serve G-d or rebel against Him. And G-d will place this to be among the man's most difficult tests and sources of temptation. For example, a king who provides for his army and servants, or princes, ministers of the king, important officials, all of who are surrounded with groups of their servants, attendants, officers, wives, and relatives. They (tend to) exert themselves to obtain money for those dependents through all types of means, regardless whether they are good or bad means.

(*Pas Lechem*: the Creator will make this thing a strong means to test him. A man is tested in this more than any other test. Because the magnitude of a test is measured by the greatness of the temptation of the evil inclination, and certainly the temptation of the evil inclination in this is exceedingly strong, to close one's hand from providing for the poor and destitute, and to not be concerned about providing their needs, thereby diminishing his wealth, as written in Devarim 15:9: "Guard yourself lest there be in your heart". This is what he meant by "tests and sources of temptation". And likewise "wives and relatives" is referring to all men [i.e. every man is master of his household and provides for his wife, children, elderly parents, etc.])

And the foolish among them will err on three fronts.

(1) In acquiring money, he will employ bad and degrading means to earn what the Creator has decreed he will earn. And if he had sought after his wealth with proper (honest) means, he would have reached his desire, and both his religious and secular affairs would have succeeded, and he would not have earned any less (money) from what the Creator had decreed for him.

(2) He thinks that all the money that reaches him is for his own support. He does not understand that the money consists of three parts: One part, for the food he needs for his own body alone, and this is something G-d assures to all living creatures to the end of its days. The second part, for the food of others, such as his wife, children, servants, employees, and the like. This (extra money) is not assured by G-d to all people (that his business will prosper to the extent that his wife and children won't themselves need to engage in some means - *PL*), but rather only to a select few, and under special conditions, and this opportunity presents itself at certain times but not at others, according to the rulings of the Creator's system of kindness and justice. Third, money to hold on to. This is money which has no benefit for the man. The man guards it and accumulates it until he bequeaths it to another or loses it. The foolish person thinks that all the money decreed for him by the Creator is for his own sustenance and physical maintenance, and so he eagerly pursues it and exerts much effort to acquire it; and it is possible that he is amassing wealth for his widow's next husband, his stepson, or for his greatest enemy.

(3) The third error is that he provides money to those (dependents) as the Creator decreed this would happen through him. But he reminds them of his favors as if he were the one who provided for them and did them a kindness. And he expects them to thank and praise him richly, and that they serve him due to them, and he becomes arrogant, haughty, and inflated of heart. He neglects to thank G-d for them (that G-d appointed him as a means to bestow good on others whereby he would be an agent for this and receive reward for it - *TL*). He thinks that if he did not give this money to them, it would remain by him, and that if he did not provide for them they would not have any money. But

really, he is the poor man, who will toil for nothing in this world and will lose his reward in the next world.

(*Marpe Lenefesh*: One can explain this to also be referring to one who realizes that it is the decree of G-d that these be provided through him. But he thinks that if there were not a decree that he provide for the poor, the abundant money would remain by him. But he errs in his outlook, because a rich man is like a funnel. If it pours down below, then we pour more up above. But if it is clogged below, we stop pouring above.)

The wise man, however, conducts himself in these three ways according to what will be proper for his religious and secular pursuits.

(*Marpe Lenefesh*: i.e. he acquires money in good and honest ways, and he is not in a rush to become rich. If he does have wealth, he will distribute it to all those who it is fitting to distribute to. He is easy-going (vatran) with his money. If he gives he is not arrogant on account of this. He doesn't desire to be praised for it, and he praises and thanks G-d who appointed him as a caretaker of many people)

His trust in what is in G-d's hands is greater than his trust in what is in his own hands because he does not know if the money in his hand is meant for his own benefit or is merely placed in his care. And thus he will gain honor in this world and receive rich reward in Olam Haba (afterlife), as written in the Psalm (112) *"Haleluy-a praiseworthy is the man who fears G-d.."* until the end of it.

(*Matanas Chelko*: The author did not discuss how much money one should leave for himself and did not mention the Halachos (laws) we find in the Shulchan Aruch on this matter. In truth this is one of the greatest trials of a rich person. For he does not know exactly how much he must give to tzedaka and how much to keep for himself.... What the Sages said of the amount of chumash (one fifth), this was said regarding every person. For even one who is not rich can give this amount. Likewise, what they wrote "one who distributes his money should not distribute more than one fifth" (Kesuvos 50a) - this refers only to average people. But one who is very rich, certainly he was not given money so that it sits in the bank. But rather, to distribute it to the poor. The Gedolim have said that all the segulos of tzedaka such as "Tzedaka (charity) saves from death" or that it "atones for one's sins" - this is only after one has already given a fifth. For, a fifth is a duty placed on every person. Therefore, only that which one gives with mesirus nefesh (self-sacrifice) has these special merits and segulas. The amount to save in the bank for a time of need depends on each person and what is the proper amount according to the way of the world... [see there are length].

WHY THE MASSES ARE FORCED TO WORK ENORMOUSLY

There are some classes of people who busy themselves in acquiring money and amassing wealth only for the love of being honored by other people, and to make a name for themselves, and no amount of money is ever enough for them. This is due to their ignorance of what will bring real honor in this world and in the next. The reason they make this error is because they see the masses honoring the wealthy, but really, this honor is motivated by a desire for what they possess and to try to get some of what is in their hands.

(*Pas Lechem*: His intent is that there are two causes why the masses honor the wealthy. (1) Because they are hoping, seeking, and longing all of their days to attain that which will bring them wealth, and since these things are very important in their thoughts, they also regard the wealthy as important. (2) Because the masses hope to draw from their hands and benefit from them, therefore they flatter them. [likewise for other things which the masses admire such as popularity, power, etc - translator])

If the masses reflected and understood that the wealthy do not have the capability nor the power either to give or to hold back to someone except to whom the Creator decreed, they would not hope to anyone besides G-d.

(*Marpe Lenefesh*: If it was decreed for this person that his money will not come from that person, then that rich person does not have the ability to give to him. Even though man has free will, the completion is not in man's hands, as written earlier. Likewise, the rich man cannot prevent this, if the Creator decreed the money will be his. G-d will arrange that the rich man will lose the money, or some other means that will cause the money to reach the hands of that person.)

Nor would they find anyone worthy of honor except for he who the Creator has distinguished with praiseworthy qualities, for which he is worthy of the Creator's honor, as written *"Those who honor Me, I will honor"* (Shmuel I 2:30).

(*Pas Lechem*: i.e. he who is worthy of the Creator's honor due to his praiseworthy traits. And since man's worth is extremely puny to be conceivably worthy of the Creator's honor, he brought a proof from the verse: "Those who honor Me, I will honor". [note: simultaneously, the verse also teaches on what will bring true honor - *Translator*])

And because, in honoring the wealthy, the masses were foolish in the causes of real honor, the Creator added to their foolishness in the causes of their requests [for money] (that they constantly seek to become rich - TL). And so they fell into great effort and tremendous toiling all of their days, while they abandoned that which is their duty to busy themselves with and to which they should hasten. Namely, fulfilling their duties to the Creator, and to thank Him for the good He bestows on them, whereby their desire (for honor - TL) would have undoubtedly been closer to them in this way, as written: *"long life is in its right, in its left wealth and honor"* (Mishlei 3:16), and *"wealth and honor is from You"* (Divrei Hayamim 29:12).

Among those who seek wealth, sometimes one reaches all his heart's desire through the means we mentioned (commerce, skilled trade, etc). For another it came through an inheritance or the like, and he thinks his wealth is due to the means, and without them, he would not have received anything, and he praises the means and not their Cause (i.e. the Creator who orchestrates all the means - *PL*).

How similar is he to a man in the desert, thirst weighing on him, who finds unclean water in a pit, and becomes full of joy. He quenches his thirst from them. And afterwards, he moves a bit further, and finds a well of pure water. He regrets on what he did previously, of drinking and quenching his thirst from the unpure water.

Similarly, for the man who became wealthy through a certain means. If this means would have failed, he would have attained it through other means, as we explained earlier and as the verse says: *"nothing can prevent G-d from saving, whether through many or through few"* (Shmuel I 14:6).

> (*Pas Lechem*: If so, all of the bitter and wearying toil he exerted himself in this means was for nothing. For it could have come to him through a light and easy business. Alternative explanation:
> *Marpe Lenefesh*: One who acquired wealth though distasteful means could have employed honest means and attained the same amount [of wealth].)

PROPER TRUST IN TIGHT FINANCIAL TIMES

And the proper way for one who trusts in G-d, when his livelihood is withheld for some day is to say in one's heart: "He who took me out (from the womb) to this world at a fixed time and moment, and did not take me out to it earlier or later, He is the One who is withholding my livelihood for a fixed time and a fixed day, because He knows what is good for me."

Likewise, when one's livelihood comes very exactly, no more than the amount for basic food, it is proper for him to reflect in his heart and tell himself: "He who prepared my sustenance at my mother's breast in my beginning, according to my need, and what was sufficient for me day by day, until He replaced it for me with something better, and (the milk's) coming exactly did not damage me at all. So too I will not at all be damaged now until the end of my days by His sending me my food in the limited, exact amount.

He will be rewarded for this, as the Creator told our ancestors in the (Sinai) desert, whose matter was in this way: *"The people shall go out each day and gather what they need for the day"* (Shemot 16:4), and *"go and call out to the ears of Jerusalem and say 'I remember for you the kindness of your youth, the love of your betrothal, when you followed Me in the wilderness, in a land that was not sown'"* (Yirmiyahu 2:2).

> (*Tov Halevanon*: The sages expounded on the reason - so that a man will always hope to G-d day by day that He will provide his daily bread [and his trust in Him will be strengthened])

Likewise, if one's livelihood comes through one means but not through any other means (that he would have preferred - *PL*), or from one place and not from any other place, or through one person and not through any other person, let one say in his heart: "He who created me in a certain form, shape, characteristic, and measure and not through any other, for my purpose and benefit, He has chosen that my livelihood come through ways suitable to my purpose and benefit, and not through any other ways." And, "He who brought me into this world at a fixed time, and through two specific people, and not through other people of the world, He has chosen for me my livelihood from a specific place and through a specific person, He made him the means to my livelihood for my benefit", as written *"G-d is righteous in all His ways"* (Tehilim 145:17).

THIRD CATEGORY - SOCIAL MATTERS

The explanation of the third category, matters of one's wife, children, household members, relatives, friends, enemies, acquaintances, those higher or lower than him among the various classes of people, the proper ways of trust in G-d is as follows. A man is necessarily in either one of two situations: either he is a stranger or he is among his family and relatives.

PROPER TRUST FOR ONE LIVING ALONE

If he is a stranger, let his companionship be with G-d during his time of loneliness, and trust in Him during his period of being a stranger. And let him contemplate that the soul is also a stranger in this world, and that all people are like strangers here, as the verse says: *"because you are strangers and temporary residents with Me"* (Vayikra 25:23). And let him reflect in his heart that all those who have relatives here, in a short time, will be left a solitary stranger. Neither relative nor son will be able to help him, and none of them will be with him (see Gate 8 ch.3 way #30 for more on this - Translator).

> (*Marpe Lenefesh*: i.e. he should reflect in his heart that it is for his benefit that he has no relatives or friends that he can enjoy with, and it is good for him so that he makes his companionship with G-d and can places his trust in Him alone. For he has no one else to trust due to his being a stranger. Furthermore, all of us are strangers because the soul, which is of divine origin, is in this world like a stranger in a strange land. And in truth, the essence of man is his soul... and further in a short while he will leave this world, and certainly then he will lay there alone without relative or savior.
>
> *Tov Halevanon*: One surrounded by family will benefit from this for only a short time. For either he will have a long life and will see the death of his children and relatives and will be left lonely and in painful solitude or if he will not live a long life, what need does he have for relatives? And this is worse than the first case.)

And afterwards, let him consider that as a stranger, he is freed from the heavy burden of maintaining relatives and fulfilling his duties towards them. He should consider this to be one of the kindnesses of the Creator towards him. For if he needed to pursue a livelihood for providing his material needs, his exertion would be lighter without a wife and children, and their absence is peace of mind for him and it is good. And if he is concerned about his interests (mitzvot) in the next world, his mind will undoubtedly be clearer and freer when he is alone.

And therefore the ascetics (pious) would leave their relatives and homes and go to the mountains, in order to focus their hearts in the service of G-d. Likewise, the prophets, during the era of prophecy, would leave their homes and live in solitude to fulfill their duties to the Creator. This is as you know from the story of Eliyahu's meeting with Elisha, which it is said of Elisha: *"twelve pairs of oxen were before him, and he was with the twelfth"* (Melachim I 19:19). And as soon as Eliyahu hinted to him a small hint (to come with him), he understood him and said *"Let me, please, kiss my father and my mother, and I will go with you"*, and afterwards, *"and he went after Eliyahu and ministered to him"*.

(*Tov Halevanon*: he left behind all of his work and separated from his mother, father, and all of his relatives and went after Eliyahu.

note: *"go to the mountains"* - such extreme asceticism is not in accordance with the teachings of Judaism and only sanctioned when practiced by such exceptional characters as Eliyahu the prophet - Rabbi Moses Hyamson zt'l [see also Gate#9])

It is said about one of the ascetics, who travelled to a country to teach its inhabitants the service of G-d. He found them all dressed in the same manner and adorned in the same way. Their graves were near their homes, and he did not see among them any women. He asked them about this and they answered him: "the reason we are all dressed alike is so that there's no noticeable difference between a rich man and a poor man and the rich man will not come to arrogance for his wealth, and the poor man will not be embarrassed of his poverty, and so that our matter above the earth should be in our eyes like our matter below the earth (i.e. in the grave where everyone is dressed the same way - TL). It is said of one of the kings that he would mix with his servants, and there was no noticeable difference between him and them, because he would conduct himself in the way of humility in his dress and adornments.

(Rav Yaakov Emden: i.e. the king would dress like them "so that his heart will not be haughty over his brothers" (Devarim

17:20). This is the way of the torah provided he does not become frivolous before them and that fear of him is over them.)

As to the reason why the graves of our dead are near our homes, they said, this is so that we encounter them and prepare ourselves for our deaths, and that we prepare our provisions for the afterlife. As to your noticing that we separated ourselves from women and children, know that we prepared for them a village near here. When one of us needs something from them, he goes to them and after obtaining his wants, returns to us. This we did because we saw how much distraction of the heart, great loss, and great exertion and strain there was when they were among us, and the great peace of mind from all of this, in separating from them, to focus on matters of the afterlife and to be repulsed by matters of this world. And their words found favor in the eyes of the ascetic, and he blessed them and commended them on their matters.

(*Pas Lechem*: He specified 4 points (distraction of the heart, great loss, great exertion and strain), the first two is the harm from desiring them, namely, when they are near, the eye sees them and the heart desires and he becomes always distracted from them, on this he wrote "distraction of the heart". And inevitably the constant desire will bring him to habitually have marital relations with them always. This causes great loss to a man's strength and health as the Rambam wrote in Hilchos Deos 4:19, on this he wrote "great loss". The latter two are the damages which come from providing for their needs (ex.big house). That when they are near, they persuade their husbands and act playfully and seek luxuries which brings to two harmful things. Namely, "great exertion" in exerting oneself to provide for their needs and "strain" of the mind in the mental distraction of providing their needs. And the Sages already said (Sotah 47a): "yetzer, child, and woman, let one's left hand push away while the right hand draws near".

Afterwards, he wrote: "to focus on matters of the afterlife and to be repulsed by matters of this world", because in distancing from them, the heart is free to think on matters of the afterlife, and also through being repulsed by this powerful lust, the heart of a man will habituate in being repulsed by the other lusts of this world.)

PROPER TRUST FOR ONE'S WIFE RELATIVES, FRIENDS, AND ENEMIES

If the one who trusts in G-d has a wife, relatives, friends, enemies, let him trust in G-d to be saved from them.

> (*Tov Halevanon*: i.e. to be saved from their burdens, namely, all those things mentioned above that a stranger is saved from.
>
> *Marpe Lenefesh*: To be saved from them by fulfilling his duties towards them.
>
> *Tov Halevanon*: Here he added the term "enemies", something he did not mention earlier regarding the man who is solitary or a stranger, because this is the normal way of the world. Namely, that the solitary man or the stranger/foreigner due to his little worldly association and his low stature, has no enemies, unlike the man with a wife, sons, relatives, friends, who has much association in the world and develops enemies due to jealousy...)

He should strive to fulfill his duties to them (provide their necessities - *PL*), to do their wishes (to also provide them with a bit more than the necessities like the nature of the world - *PL*), to be wholehearted with them (to provide their needs willingly, not like one forced to do so - *PL*). He should refrain from causing any harm to them, try to promote what is good for them. He should deal faithfully towards them in all matters, and teach them the ways that will be beneficial for them in their religious matters and the secular ways [which will benefit them] in the service of the Creator, as written (Vayikra 19:18) *"you shall love your neighbor as yourself.."*, and *"do not hate your brother in your heart"* (ibid). Do not do this out of hope for future benefits from them or to pay them back for past benefits. Nor should you do this out of love of being honored or praised by them, or out of desire to rule over them - but rather with the sole motive to fulfill the commandment of the Creator, and to guard His covenant and precepts over them. (i.e. to see to it that they guard the covenant of G-d and His commandments - *TL*)

The person whose motive in fulfilling their wishes is one of the [reprehensible] motives we mentioned above, will not obtain what he wants from them in this world. He will weary himself for nothing, and will lose his reward in the afterlife (since his intent was not l'Shem Shamayim - *PL*). But if his sole motive is to serve G-d, the Al-mighty will help them to make a return to him in this world, and G-d will place his praise in their mouths and they will hold him in high esteem, and he will attain the great reward in Olam Haba (afterlife), as the Al-mighty said to Shlomo *"also what you did not ask, I will give you, also wealth and honor"* (Melachim 3:13).

(*Pas Lechem*: Corresponding to "do not do this out of hope for future benefits, etc.", he wrote: "the Al-mighty will help them to make a return to him".
Corresponding to "Nor should you do this out of love of being honored or praised by them", he wrote: "and G-d will place his praise in their mouths".
Corresponding to "(nor should you do this) out of desire to rule over them", he wrote: "and they will hold him in high esteem", that he will seem great and awe-inspiring in their eyes and automatically they will do whatever he says.
Therefore without intending to, indirectly, he attained all of their benefits in this world, similar to what our sages said (Nedarim 62a): "study the Torah out of love, and in the end, the honor will come". And his primary reward will be in Olam Haba)

PROPER TRUST FOR BENEFITING FROM OTHERS

But the ways of trust in G-d in dealing with those above him or below him in the various classes of men is as follows. The proper way to act when one needs to request some benefit of someone above or below him is to trust in G-d, and to consider them as means of obtaining what he needs, just like one makes the working and sowing of the land a means of obtaining his food. If

G-d wishes to support him through it, He will make the seeds sprout, grow, and multiply, and one does not thank the land for this, but rather, he thanks the Creator alone. And if the Al-mighty will not desire to supply him through it, the land will not produce, or it will produce but be struck by damaging things, and one does not blame the land.

So too, when he seeks something from one of them, it should be equal in his eyes whether the person he asked is weak or strong, and he should trust in G-d for its completion.

> (*Pas Lechem*: i.e. that he does not trust more in his heart that his request will be completed if he had asked a strong person than if he had asked a weak person, since he believes that the man is only an intermediary and that G-d is the one actually doing it.)

And if it was completed through one of them, let him thank the Creator who fulfilled his desire, and thank the person through whom it was done for his good will towards him, and that the Creator brought his benefit through him. And it is known that the Creator does not bring good except through the tzadikim (righteous), and it is rare that He brings a loss through them, as the sages said *"merit occurs through the meritorious and guilt through the guilty"* (Bava Basra 119b), and the verse *"No wrong shall be caused for the righteous"* (Mishlei 12:21 - Rashi "No sin will chance before him inadvertently").

> (*Tov Halevanon*: i.e. perhaps you will say, if the matter is so (that G-d is doing it and the person is only an intermediary) why should I thank a person who benefits me, since he is forced by G-d and does good to me without choice due to the decree of G-d? (Answer:) you are obligated to thank him nevertheless since he is the one G-d chose to cause the good and G-d brings good through the righteous and faithful before Him...)

And if his request is not accomplished through them, one should not blame them, and not consider it due to their being lax in it. Rather he should thank the Al-mighty who chose what is best for him in this, and praise them according to his knowledge of their efforts to fulfill his will, even though the matter was not completed according to his will and their desire. Similarly, one should act with his acquaintances and friends, his business associates, employees and partners.

If someone higher or lower than himself requests from him to do something for them, he should wholeheartedly use every means to do it, and apply his mind to do the matter, provided one is capable of doing it and that the person who requested it is worthy that he exerts himself on his behalf (but if the person is wicked, refrain from it as he wrote in the end of gate #3 - *ML*). And after this, he should trust in the Al-mighty for its completion. If G-d completes it through him, and makes him the cause for benefiting another, he should thank G-d for this privilege. If G-d withholds this from him, and he is not capable of doing it, he should not blame himself, and he should inform the person that he was not lax in doing it, provided that he indeed exerted himself to do it.

PROPER TRUST FOR DEALING WITH ENEMIES

But for one's enemies, those jealous of him, those who seek to harm him, he should trust in G-d regarding their matters. He should bear their contempt, and should not treat them back in the same way.

> (*Marpe Lenefesh*: As the sages said (Yoma 23a see Rashi, Rosh Hashana 17a): "he who forgoes (overlooks) his honor when it is slighted will merit that all his transgressions be forgiven")

Rather he should pay them back with kindness, and to try to benefit them as much as he possibly can, and to remember in his heart that only G-d has the ability to benefit or harm him.

> (*Translator*: I once heard a lecture by Rabbi Nissan Kaplan of the Mir Yeshiva where he said that this method is one of the most powerful ways to work on trust. In order to internalize trust, one must do physical actions in this world, namely paying back evil with good. He says that getting into the habit of doing this, is one of the ways to build trust in the most

effective way.

Rabbi Avigdor Miller zt'l also says getting in the habit of always thanking G-d for the good and the bad also builds trust.

If his enemy becomes a means to harm him, he should judge them favorably and suspect that it is due to himself or his past deeds from his bad start in life towards G-d. He should plead to the Al-mighty and seek from Him to atone for his sins, and then his enemies will become his friends, as the wise man said *"when G-d is pleased with a man's way, even his enemies will make peace with him"* (Mishlei 16:7).

(*Matanas Chelko*: the main trust in these matters is as the Chazon Ish wrote: "to abstain doing [bad] things to those who did bad to him" (Emuna U'Bitachon 2:2). For the primary denial of trust is to do [bad] against one who did bad to him or vexed him, as written in the Sefer Hachinuch regarding the commandment not to exact revenge which is one of the roots of faith. Therefore, the author wrote that it is included in the commandment of "love your fellow as yourself". For denial of G-d is recognized and manifest when one exacts revenge on someone who did bad to him. He forgets the great principle of the Ramban (end of parsha Bo): "if he does G-d's commandments, G-d will reward him with success. But if he transgresses them, G-d will afflict him with punishments - everything is from divine decree."

Rabbi Yaakov Emden zt'l: This matter requires great investigation. We find many verses supporting this such as "Do not say: 'I will repay evil'; but wait on the L-ord, and He shall save you" (Mishlei 20:22), "If your enemy is hungry, give him bread to eat; and if he is thirsty, give him water to drink" (ibid 25:21). Likewise, we find by King David especially with Saul in the cave and with his garment, and like Saul said to him (Shmuel 24:19): "And you have shown today how you have dealt well with me, how the L-rd delivered me into your hand, and you did not kill me; For when a man finds his enemy, does he send him away safely? And may the L-rd repay you with goodness for what you have done to me on this day". And in Tehilim (35:13) "But as for me, when they (my enemies) were ill, my clothing was sackcloth", and (ibid 38:14) "Thus I was as a man that hears not, and in whose mouth are no reproofs (when others were mocking me)", and (ibid 37:7) "Be silent before the L-ord, and wait patiently for him: fret not yourself because of him who prospers in his way, because of the man who brings wicked devices to pass", and (ibid 62:5) "My soul, wait you only upon G-d; for my expectation is from Him", and many more like this.

On the other hand, we find many verses which contradict this, especially by King David for he sought to exact furious revenge from Naval merely for refraining from doing good to him. Likewise, he pleaded G-d to exact revenge on his enemies, as he said: (ibid 41:11) "be gracious to me and raise me up, so that I may repay them", and (ibid 28:4) "Give them according to their deeds and according to the evil of their endeavors", and he complained (119:84) "How many are Your servant's days? When will You execute justice upon my pursuers?", and many more like this. He even praised revenge in saying: (58:11) "The righteous shall rejoice when he sees the vengeance".

And his overlooking of Shimi in saying (Shmuel II 16:10) "G-d told him to curse" is not an indication since he was then in great troubles, and he humbled himself and accepted the humiliation as an atonement, thereby bearing the pain in exchange for the punishment fitting for him for the event with Batsheva. And in the end when Shimi sought forgiveness, it was fitting for him to pardon him due to the need of the time and also since one who admits and repents is treated with mercy (by G-d). Even so, David guarded the matter and paid him back through his son Shlomo. And it does not appear correct to say that whenever scripture praises revenge it is referring to the gentile enemies of G-d and His people (who come to wage war, etc.). Likewise, Yirmiyahu pleaded for revenge from the men of Anatot, who were Kohanim of his own family, in saying (Yirmiyahu 15:15) "avenge me of my persecutors; take me not away in your long-suffering". We must answer all this by saying that everything varies according to the severity of the matter and the greatness of the wrongdoing. (translator - and the author here is speaking about most cases which are usually petty matters)

Afterwards, he wrote: "He should plead to the Al-mighty and seek from Him to atone for his sins", similar to what David did in the event with Shimi. Then, "his enemies will become his friends" as what happened with Yaakov and Eisav or the tribes with Yosef, and obviously with Shimi.

FOURTH CATEGORY - Duties of the heart and limbs which don't affect others

PROPER TRUST IN THE FREE WILL TO SERVE G-D

The explanation of the fourth category, matters of duties of the heart and of the limbs which only benefit or harm oneself, for example, fasting, praying, dwelling in a sukka, taking a lulav, wearing tzitzis, observing the Sabbath and the holidays, refraining from sins. This category also includes all of the duties of the heart since their performance does not affect others, and their benefit or harm is limited only to oneself and is not shared by others. I will explain the proper way of trust in the Al-mighty in all of these, and I ask the Al-mighty to teach me the truth, in His mercy.

(*Pas Lechem*: In his examples, he first wrote "fasting" and "praying", since these mitzvos are logical, and were practiced before the giving of the torah. Adam also fasted and prayed for his sin. Afterwards, he gave the examples of received mitzvot, and started with "sukka" since of all the mitzvot which apply today, it is the reminder of the clouds of glory in the desert (i.e. the Exodus from Egypt). He said lulav before tzitzis since it is preceded in the torah... [see there for more details]

Matanas Chelko: "I ask the Al-mighty..." it seems from the author's words that the following branch of trust is the most difficult to explain. Since we don't find that he uttered a

prayer like this anywhere else in the book when explaining
trust. Perhaps, it is because he is explaining the foundations
of free will.)

Any human action which is either service [of G-d] or sin can only
take place if three factors occur. (1) the choice in heart and mind
(i.e. a thought that it is fitting to do this thing - *ML*). (2) The intent
and resolve to do what one chose. (3) The endeavoring to
complete the act with one's physical limbs and to bring it into
actuality.

[Of these three factors,] two are not beyond our control, namely,
(1) the choice of service or sin and (2) intent and resolve to carry
out the choice. For these, trusting in G-d would be a mistake and
a foolishness, because the Creator left free choice in our hands
whether to serve Him or rebel against Him, as written "...[life and
death I have set before you] and you shall choose life" (Devarim
30:19).

(*Tov Halevanon*: If a man does not choose to pursue doing
good and to refrain from sins, and instead trusts in G-d that
He will prepare that good deeds will come his way and that
G-d will distance from him the causes which lead to sins -
this is a great mistake.)

But the bringing out of the act into actuality, He did not leave in
our hands, but rather, made it depend on external means which
sometimes are available and sometimes are not.

(*Tov Halevanon*: For example, fasting and prayer, perhaps
his body will be too weak, or sukkah and lulav, perhaps he
will not be able to obtain the sukkah wood or the lulav... Or to
give charity, he needs to have money, and to encounter a
proper poor man, etc. These external means are not in our
free choice nor in the desire of G-d, but rather occur by
encounter and opportunity. Only that for good deeds, there is
a bit of siyata dishmaya (Divine assistance) as our sages
taught (Shabbat 104a): "if one comes to purify himself, he is
helped", but "if one comes to defile himself, he is given an
opening" (ibid 104a), i.e. that the means are left to chance
[Translator: not that G-d pushes him to defile himself but

rather He withdraws His providence and leaves the person to chance as written in the introduction to this gate])

If in choosing to serve the Al-mighty, one would trust in Him and think to himself: "I will not choose the service of G-d nor attempt to do any part of it until He chooses what is good for me of it" - he has already strayed from the straight path, and slipped his feet away from the proper way. Because the Creator has already commanded us to choose in matters of His service, and to intend and make efforts towards it, with complete, wholehearted resolve for the sake of His great Name, and He has informed us that this is the proper way for our welfare in this world and in the next.

(Translator: His great Name refers to G-d as He manifests Himself to us. This is explained earlier in gate#1. We use the term "His Name" because G-d Himself is too beyond for us to even speak about.)

If the necessary means are available to us, so that we are capable of accomplishing the work in G-d's service which we chose to do, then we will receive the great reward for choosing it, for the intent and resolve to do it, and for completing the actions by our physical limbs. But if its accomplishment with the physical limbs is withheld from us, then we will receive reward for our choice and intent to do it, as we previously explained (in ch.3), and similarly for punishment of sins.

(*Tov Halevanon*: And if you ask, how can this be a mitzvah if there was no act done yet? For this he said that the completion of the act is not essential to the mitzvah. Even though the mitzvah is not accomplished, he will receive reward for the choice and resolve to do it. But if the act is completed, the reward is greater, and likewise for punishments of sins.)

The difference between the service of G-d and secular activities in this world, regarding trust in G-d, is as follows. For secular matters, it was not revealed to us which one of all the means is best and most beneficial for us nor the ways in which some course is more harmful and worse than other courses. We do not know which particular trade is best suited for us and most fitting for us in obtaining money, preserving health, and for general well-being. Nor do we know which business sector, which journey to undertake, or which other worldly endeavors will be successful if we engage in them.

Therefore, it follows that we must put our trust in the Al-mighty that He will help us choose and carry out what is the best choice for us, provided that we apply ourselves (in the means which are fitting to attain this thing - *PL*) and that we plead to Him to arouse in our hearts to make the good and proper choice for ourselves. (then after these two things we can have in our hearts the trust mentioned - *PL*)

> (*Tov Halevanon*: Lest you ask: "if so, (that in the choice and resolve in the service of G-d, I must not trust in G-d) then also I must not trust in Him for matters of my livelihood. If so, why did the author say earlier that one should "submit himself to the course the Creator has decreed for him...". On this he answered, that there is a big difference between the two...
>
> *Marpe Lenefesh*: He gave a reason for this difference, namely, "it was not revealed to us which means is best...", and we don't know what to do, whether engaging in this trade or that business will be best for us or maybe in something else. And as the sages said (Berachos 33b) "everything is in the hands of Heaven (G-d), except for fear of Heaven")

But the service of G-d is not like this, because G-d has already taught us the proper ways for it, commanded us to choose it, and gave us the ability to do it. If we then plead to Him in the choice we should make, and trust in Him that He will reveal to us what is good for us, we will be mistaken in our words (of prayer) and foolish in our trust. For He already taught us the proper way which will be good for us in this world and in the next, as written: *"G-d has commanded us to fulfill all of these statutes, to fear the L-ord, our G-d, for our good, all of our days"* (Devarim 6:24). And regarding the reward in Olam Haba *"we will be rewarded, if we are careful to observe"* (Devarim 6:25).

Furthermore, in secular matters, sometimes a good means changes to become a bad means and vice versa, while for service of G-d and transgression it is not so. Matters of good and evil do not switch positions and never change.

> (*Marpe Lenefesh*: Furthermore, how can we charge our mind to choose this business or this trade? Many times we find one person becomes rich through this business or trade and it is good for him, while another person does not profit at all from it and it is bad for him. If so, there is no way for us to know, rather only that which G-d puts in our hearts [to choose] is for our good. We find many verses which teach this such as (Mishlei 19:21) "There are many plans in a man's heart but the counsel of the L-ord - that shall stand", and "A man's heart plans his way: but the L-ord directs his steps" (Mishlei 16:9), and "A man's steps are directed by the L-ord; how then can anyone understand his own way" (ibid 20:24), and many more verses. But the actions in the service of G-d that are good, namely, fulfilling the commandments - this is good forever and never changes. Likewise the negative commandments are always bad.
> (another explanation)
> *Tov Halevanon*: That even though it appears good, it is possible that in the end it will lead to destruction, and the opposite, what appears evil and bitter in one's eyes may turn out in the end to be a great salvation. And like our sages said (Berachos 54a): "a person should bless on the bad, like he blesses on the good...")

Hence, for religious acts, trust in G-d is proper only in the completion stage of the act. After choosing it wholeheartedly and faithfully and after the second stage of resolving and making efforts to do it with a pure heart, and with intent to do it for the sake of His great Name. With this, we are obligated to beseech Him to help us in it, and to teach us on it, as written: *"lead me in Your truth and teach me"* (Tehilim 25:5), and *"lead me in the path of Your commandments for I desired it"* (Tehilim 119:35), and *"I have chosen the way of truth, I have placed Your ordinances before me"* (Tehilim 119:30), and *"I have clung to Your testimonies; O L-ord; put me not to shame"* (Tehilim 119:31), and *"And take not the word of truth utterly out of my mouth; for I have hoped in Your judgments"* (Tehilim 119:43).

> (*Rabbi Yaakov Emden*: "we are obligated to beseech Him to help us in it" also against the Yetzer (evil inclination) since: "every day a person's evil inclination rises powerfully against him and seeks to slay him...Were it not for the Holy One blessed be He who helps him, a man would not be able [to contend] with it" (Kidushin 30b).
>
> *Pas Lechem*: "after choosing it" means: to make a strong decision in his mind to not budge from it.
> "wholeheartedly" means: not hesitantly.
> "faithfully" means: choosing to do it without outside interests.
> "with a pure heart" means: making efforts to do it without outside interests but rather "for the sake of His great Name".
>
> *Tov Halevanon*: "and with intent to do it for the sake of His great Name" - i.e. with all this, everything goes by the intent as our sages said (Nazir 23b): "a sin lishma (for the sake of G-d) is greater than a mitzvah that is not lishma.
> "to teach us on it" means to remove the veil of foolishness from our eyes and to strengthen our choice towards Him so that we may also know the ways of His service and by which way we should seek it.)

All these verses demonstrate that the psalmist's service of G-d was his own choice. He prayed to G-d for two things only:
(1) To wholly devote his heart and to strengthen his choice in the service of G-d by distancing the distractions of the world from his heart and eyes, as he said *"unite my heart to fear Your Name"* (ibid 86:11) and *"uncover my eyes that I may gaze at the wonders of Your torah"* (Tehilim 119:18), *"turn away my eyes from beholding vanity"* (ibid, 119:37), *"incline my heart towards Your torah and not to unjust gain"* (ibid, 119:36), and many more.

> (*Pas Lechem*: "To wholly devote his heart" means: that his thoughts be only in G-d's service, not in the vain worldly desires and to strengthen his choice that it be enduringly set and firmly established

Matanas Chelko: "to strengthen his choice" - prayer is to strengthen one's choice, i.e. before the act is completed. For example, one who has decided to go learn torah in the synagogue, it is possible that he will be met with many distractions along the way. He may see some event or hear something, or some idea enters his mind. Each of these can potentially change his plan or weaken his resolve so he does not learn properly. Therefore, one must pray even after the decision and resolve in order to strengthen one's choice against the distractions. This is the important principle Rabeinu is teaching us - the purpose of prayer for spiritual things is to strengthen one's will.)

(2) To strengthen him physically to be able to complete the acts of service of G-d. This is what is meant *"lead me in the path of Your commandments"* (119:35), *"support me and I will be saved"* (119:117), and many more like this. And I will explain in this gate which factors help and harm these things, and the proper path in it, with G-d's help.

Matanas Chelko: To summarize, in matters that one does not know the proper path, and with what should he engage in, he should trust in G-d and pray to G-d that He will put in his heart the will of what to do and how to do it. On the other hand, for things which he already knows are proper and that he should do them, such as the study of Torah and performance of commandments, it is not proper to beseech G-d to give him the will to do them. But one can beseech G-d to strengthen his will in them, remove the obstructions from doing them, and ask Him that he merits to accomplish his good choice to fulfill them.

A note on the matter of free will: Rabeinu (our teacher) included in his words the foundation of what is free will. Those who think free will means that a person can do what he wants - are mistaken. For behold, whether for physical or spiritual matters, one does not have the ability to do what he wants - for everything is done solely by divine decree. And even for doing a commandment or a sin - even though he wants to do it, it is possible that sometimes G-d will prevent him from doing it. Rather, free will means the will to do. A person has free will to choose what he wants to do. But to bring this thought to actuality is only in G-d's hands.

If we go deeper in this, we will see that in truth, even the will to do something is not "free will". For behold, even an animal has the will to do what it wants. The animal wants to eat, sleep, kick - and does it. So too, a man wants to eat, sleep, etc. and does it. If so, what is the difference between man and animal? The answer is that a man's free will is that he has the ability to refrain from doing what he wants.

This is the difference between man and animal. The animal cannot refrain from doing what it wants. That which its nature wants to do, it does. It does not have the power to refrain from doing what it wants. But a man has been granted the ability to refrain from doing what his nature wants to do. If an animal lusts for something, it does not have the ability to restrain itself from fulfilling this lust and will. A human being on the other hand, can lust for physical things. But he has the power to refrain from fulfilling that will and lust which his nature pushes him to do. This is true free will - to form in his being, through his intellect, the will and desire to overcome his natural desires.

The root of free will is fear of G-d. That which the torah says "you shall choose life" (Deut. 30:19), which implies man has free will, this refers to the free will to acquire fear of G-d. Namely, to form in his being the will to fulfill the will of G-d instead of pursuing the fulfillment of his natural will. This is free will. All the other things he does stem from the tendency of his nature, just like an animal. Hence, it is possible for a man to spend his entire life without ever using his free will even once! Because free will is that which a person creates and forms by himself through fear [of G-d], a new will to stand up against his animalistic and natural will, in order to fulfill the will of G-d. This is what our sages said (Berachos 33b): "everything is in the hands of Heaven except the fear of Heaven". For only through the power of fear of G-d that a person has can he overcome and stand up against what was already decreed from Heaven, namely, his natural will and powers.)

FIFTH CATEGORY - Duties of the limbs which affect others

The fifth category: physical duties which affect others whether beneficially or harmfully, such as giving charity, maaser (tithes), teaching wisdom, commanding others to do good, warning them against evil, returning loans on faith, keeping a secret, speaking well of others, good activities, honoring parents, bringing the wicked back to G-d, instructing/advising others what will be good for them, pitying the poor and treating them with mercy, patiently bearing their contempt when arousing them to the service G-d, inspiring them to hope for the reward [in doing good], and instilling in them fear of punishment [for doing bad].

The proper way of trust in G-d for these, is for one to keep in mind all these and similar acts, resolve and make efforts to practice them, according to what we previously explained in the fourth category. Namely, regarding the duty when choosing (in these things - PL) to have the sole intent of drawing near to G-d alone; not for acquiring a name or honor among human beings, nor out of hope to receive reward from them, nor to try to rule over them. And after one has done his utmost, he should trust in G-d in the completion of the acts which he undertook, according to what G-d wants from us (that we do His will, accordingly He will help us to complete what we undertook - *ML*).

In all of this, one should be careful to hide his deeds as much as possible from those who do not need to know. Because if it is kept hidden, the reward will be greater than if it becomes known. And that which he is unable to hide, let him remember the important general principle which we explained, namely, that neither benefit nor harm can come from the created things, except by permission of the Creator.

(*Pas Lechem*: If he cannot hide it and therefore, he is afraid lest the yetzer put in his heart ulterior motives, as before, then let him remember...

Manoach Halevavos: If he is unable to hide he will be mocked by the mockers, or obstructed from completing it due to their h. that the poor man he benefits will receive shame, concerned thereby refraining from the good deed. Ratne. "remember the important general principle...", and that it is not in the ability of others to obstruct him, or hamper him, and the mockery will not damage him. Likewise, the shame of the poor man will not harm him, with G-d's help.)

When the Creator completes a mitzvah (commandment) through him (that G-d benefits another person through him - *PL*), he should consider that this is a favor bestowed on him from the Creator. He should not rejoice if other people praise him for doing it, nor desire that they honor him for it. For this will bring him to become proud in his actions, and his purity of heart and motive towards G-d will be ruined, thereby his deeds will be spoiled and his reward for it will be lost. I will explain this later on in its proper Gate (in #6 the gate of submission - *PL*) with G-d's help.

(*Pas Lechem*: "his deeds will be spoiled" - G-d will not accept his deeds and also he will lose his reward.

Marpe Lenefesh: "his reward for it will be lost" since he had pleasure and praise for his deed, he already received his reward for this.)

SIXTH CATEGORY - reward in this world and the next

The explanation of the sixth category, regarding the reward in this world and the next which one merits for his good deeds in this world, is divided into two parts. (1) Sometimes for an act, the reward is given in this world only or it is given in the next world only. (2) Sometimes the reward is given in both worlds for one act.

This was not explained to us clearly. However, the Creator guaranteed to His people a general reward for general good behavior, but He did not specify the details of reward in this world act of service like He did regarding the punishments in orld for transgressions. For example, He specified which ices warrant capital punishment by stoning (i.e. falling from a ight), burning, decapitation, or strangulation, or 40 lashes, death (through G-d's providence), premature death (karet), monetary fines - two, four or five fold, monetary damages by ox, pit, tooth, fire, damaging a man, embarrassing by seizing, slander, and other offences. But regarding the reward and punishment in the afterlife, the prophet [Moshe] did not explain anything for several reasons.

One of these is that the semblance of the soul without the body is foreign to us, and even less known is what the soul in that state would take pleasure in or suffer from. However, this was explained to one who understood such things, as G-d spoke to Yehoshua (the high priest) (who G-d granted special understanding into divine matters - *PL*) "I will give you a place to walk among these (angels) that stand" (Zecharia 3:7), and this was not referring to when the soul is joined to the body. But rather, was a hint to what would happen after death where the soul, in its simple, ethereal state, divested from and no longer using the body, resumes the form of the angels, after it had been purified and made radiant when its deeds were good in this world.

(*Pas Lechem*: "the soul in its simple, ethereal state":
"simple" - in that it is divested of the entanglement of its physicality.
"ethereal" - in that its essence is extremely sublime in spiritual constitution.
"after it had been purified and made radiant when its deeds were good in this world" - i.e. the soul will attain this through purifying itself in this world. He specified two terms "purified" and "made radiant" because there are two evils which the soul is susceptible to from the entanglement and sickness of physicality. One, that the physicality defiles it by causing it to do bad deeds and sins. Two, the defilement from the superfluous desires (for excessive food, speech, tranquility, etc. see Gate 3). Even though the latter does not cause "corrosion" on it as much as much as sins do, nevertheless,

it will not escape from some defilement and filth which it absorbs from the physical...

Marpe Lenefesh: The above account of Yehoshua Kohen Gadol was entirely a spiritual vision, as it is written there: "And he showed me Yehoshua the high priest standing before the angel of the L-ord..." Certainly those standing there are spiritual beings, and when he will "walk among them", certainly it means without a physical body.

Tov Halevanon: I will give you a place to walk among these (angels) that stand" - means that he will have kiyum (ability to exist) in the world of angels.)

Another reason is that the explanation of reward and punishment in the next world was received by the people from the prophets and can be derived by the wise (in every generation, in addition to the transmitted tradition - *PL*). And the explanation was left out of books just like much of the explanation of the positive and negative commandments were left out, relying on the transmission from the oral tradition.

(*Marpe Lenefesh*: The prophets would explain it to them by heart, just like most of the torah and the explanation of the commandments were transmitted orally by heart, due to many sound reasons.

Marpe Lenefesh: "can be derived by the wise" - since obviously the main reward and punishment is in the next world, since, behold, in this world life is short and its good does not last, and there is not one person in the world who is completely in enjoyment, without any sadness, worry, or fear to hinder his joy. If so, one who does the will of G-d in this world will certainly be rewarded according to His infinite ability and goodness, which cannot be imagined in this world, and certainly this is in the next world which is eternal and all good. See the Sefer Hayashar for a detailed explanation of this.)

Another reason is that the people were foolish and of little understanding (when they left Egypt) something which is not hard to see in the verses.

> (*Pas Lechem*: Their foolishness was to such a great extent that it was not hard to see from what is written in the Torah, namely, their hearts' craving for the desires such as asking for meat and other complaints, and little understanding in fundamental matters of purpose, as we see from the incident of the golden calf or their complaints regarding the spies and the congregation of Korach.)

The Creator conducted Himself with them like a father who has mercy on his young son, when he wants to discipline him slowly and gently (so as not to overload him, so too the Creator did not want to inform them of the punishments in the afterlife which are very harsh - *PL*), as written *"Yisrael is a child, and I loved him"* (Hoshea 11:1). When a father wants to educate his young son in the wisdom with which he will attain exalted levels, and the youth is not capable of understanding them at that time, if he tries to induce him, saying "bear the hard discipline and the learning, in order that you later reach the great levels", the son would not have the patience to bear this, and would not listen to his father, because he does not understand them.

But if the father promised him with what is pleasurable right away, whether food and drink, fine clothing and a nice wagon, or the like, and warned him [that if he did not heed he would suffer] what will cause him immediate pain such as hunger, nakedness, spankings or the like, and gave him clear proofs and tangible evidence, so as to impress these promises and warnings in his son's mind and the truth of his statements, it will be easy for the son to bear the strain of the discipline and to endure its tedious work.

And when he becomes a young man and his intellect strengthens, he will understand the intent of the discipline he was put through (the exalted levels - *PL*) and turn towards them. He will think little of the sweetness of pleasures which he had earlier been so eager to run towards. This kind of education was a kindness toward him. (i.e. this conduct to motivate him initially through sweet things, etc. as before, was due to the father's mercy on him - *PL*)

> (*Pas Lechem*: Two forms of strain are needed in the study of
> [torah] wisdom. One, that a person is required to be
> imprisoned in the prison of the study halls of wisdom.
> Namely, to be constantly entrenched at the feet of the sages,
> as the talmud says: "it (the torah) is not to be found among
> merchants and dealers" (Eruvin 55a), and likewise in
> Shabbos (120a) on the verse "I will not be a chovesh (binder
> up)" [the talmud expounds:] "I will not be of those who shut
> themselves up in the Beit Hamidrash (house of torah study)".
> Two, the strain of the learning itself, as the talmud says
> (Sanhedrin 26b): "why is the torah called tushia (in Isaiah
> 28:29)? Because it weakens the strength of man [through
> constant study]". Corresponding to these two the author
> used two expressions "(1) bear the hard discipline and (2)
> the learning", and correspondingly he wrote two expressions:
> "(1) the son would not have the patience to bear this, (2) and
> would not listen to his father", "because he does not
> understand them" - he does not understand the exalted
> levels which this will lead him to.
> Afterwards he wrote: "it will be easy for the son to bear the
> strain of the discipline and to endure its tedious work"
> corresponding to these two.)

Similarly, the Creator encouraged his people with promises of
rewards and threatened them with punishments that would come
soon i.e. in this world - PL. For He knew that after they would be
strongly established in the service, their foolishness regarding
reward and punishment here on earth would shed (i.e. that which
they served primarily for reward in this world [would shed] - *PL*)
and their intent in the service would be to Him, and they would
direct their conduct for Him. And in this way, we can explain all of
the physical forms ascribed to the Creator in scripture.

> (*Pas Lechem*: "and their intent in the service would be to
> Him" refers to the intent in each specific act, that they would
> direct their intent to G-d in every act that they do. And for the
> general conduct in the service he wrote: "they would direct
> their conduct towards Him", that all of their aspirations in
> their conduct would be to cling to Him.

Marpe Lenefesh: that which scripture ascribes physical form to G-d, such as "the hand of G-d" (Shemos 9:3), "the eyes of G-d" (Devarim 11:12), is also for this reason - so that everyone will understand together, the wise man and the fool, that there is a Creator and Master, as explained at length in Gate #1 chapter 10)

Another reason, is that a man does not become worthy of the reward of Olam Haba (the next world) due to his good deeds alone (since the reward is infinitely great - *TL*). Rather he is deemed by G-d worthy of it due to two things besides his good deeds. (1) That he teaches other people the service of G-d, and guides them to do good, as written "they who bring merit to the public shall be as the stars forever" (Daniel 12:3). And also, "to them that rebuke shall be delight, and on them will come the blessing of the good" (Mishlei 24:25). And when the industrious man will combine the reward for those who he brought merit, with the reward for his own good deeds, and the reward for the faith in his heart and patient acceptance [of G-d's will] - he will be deemed by the Creator worthy of the reward of Olam Haba. (i.e. if he also brings merit to others in addition to his own piety, then certainly he is worthy of the reward, as written: "to them that rebuke shall be delight" - *ML*)

(*Tov Halevanon*: (from Gate 8 ch.3) those who rebuke others on their wickedness, the delight of G-d and the blessing of G-d will come to them, and certainly for one who rebukes himself for his wickedness, his reward will be greater and more intense.

Matanas Chelko: To merit entering the world to come, one must have earned the mitzva of bringing merit to the public. After he has merited to enter there, his state and level will be according to his specific service of G-d. But one who properly performed the commandments and became a tzadik but did not bring any person to torah, he does not have the key to the world to come. (See there at length for an explanation. A summary is that one can be paid all his reward in this world for all commandments but not for

sanctifying G-d's Name which comes through bringing others
close to torah. see there.)

(2) The second factor is a kindness from the Al-mighty, and a
generosity and goodness, as written *"to You, G-d, is kindness,
for You pay a man according to his deeds"* (Tehilim 62:13) (i.e.
even if one has only his own good deeds [and did not bring
others to the good], G-d will bestow on him good reward in Olam
Haba - *TL*).

The reason for this, is that even if a man's good deeds are
numerous like the sand of the seashore, it would not weigh
enough to cover even one favor the Creator has bestowed on
him in this world. All the more so, if he has committed any sins.
For if the Creator will hold a man strictly to account for his
obligation of gratitude, all of his good deeds would be cancelled
and wiped out by even the smallest favor the Creator has done
for him, and that which the Creator owes him will not amount to
anything. Hence, that which the Creator rewards a person for his
good deeds is to be regarded as a Divine grace to him.

> (*Tov Halevanon*: "it is a kindness of the Almighty" - i.e. to
> bestow good reward (Olam Haba) to a Tzadik (righteous
> man) due to his own good deeds alone, even if he does not
> teach others and rebukes them. Although, justice demands
> that a person be held accountable for the sin of his fellow
> since "all of Yisrael are arevim (responsible) for each other"
> (Shevuot 39a) for visible matters (provided one can
> effectively rebuke the other person) and also since we have
> been commanded to teach others and rebuke them as a
> positive commandment. Nevertheless, from the abundant
> kindness of G-d which has intensified on us, G-d does not
> withhold His reward in Olam Haba. Likewise, even if one
> teaches others and rebukes his fellow back to the good, it is
> still, [strictly speaking,] not enough to merit the reward of
> Olam Haba which is infinitely great, were it not for His
> kindness... Hence the torah and the prophets did not mention
> the rewards of Olam Haba in the section of the covenant and
> the rebuke (Parsha Bechukosai, Ki Tavo, Shema) since,
> according to justice, a man does not deserve this reward,

and it is sufficient to give man reward in this world. Hence, the torah only mentioned what is proper according to justice. Similarly, our sages taught: "prophecy was asked 'what should be the punishment for the sinner?', It replied: 'the soul which sins shall die'. 'The torah was asked, etc.', it replied: 'let him bring an Asham (temple offering) and be atoned', G-d was asked, etc. He replied: 'let him come and do teshuva (repentance)'. Understand this. And since the torah did not mention the rewards, it likewise did not mention the punishments despite that it is a debt he must pay according to his sins.

Marpe Lenefesh: The Sh'la wrote (page 52b): "Consider an analogy of one who [severely] broke his leg or blinded an eye, and a great doctor came and through his great expertise, healed him for free, or even for pay. Wouldn't he love him greatly all of his days, and nothing the doctor asked of him would be difficult for him? Behold, G-d gave a person hands, feet - all of his limbs, and sustains him and watches over him, and gave him a soul so that he can come to immortality..." see there for more. And the author already wrote in Gate#2 ch.5 on some of the favors that G-d did to us from our first existence in this world until today. He who places them always before his eyes - then, his heart will become fiery (impassioned) towards G-d, yisborach.)

The punishment in both worlds, however, is through truth and justice, and it is a debt a man must pay. Yet here too the Creator's loving-kindness is extended to us in both worlds, as written *"to You, G-d, belongs loving-kindness"* (Tehilim 62:13), and *"the compassionate One will atone for sin, and will not destroy"* (Tehilim 78:38).

(*Tov Halevanon*: G-d's kindness here means that G-d waits for him always in this world and gives him time to repent, and if he repents, even if it is just before his death, G-d will exempt him from the punishments of Olam Haba (i.e. but if not, then no sins are overlooked and must be punished in order to pardon the person as will be explained later. - Translator)

Marpe Lenefesh: The kindness is that He pays man some punishment in this world with easy suffering (instead of paying him in the next world with far worse suffering), and also slowly, slowly one at a time, not in furious wrath, as written: "Only you did I love above all the families of the earth; therefore, I will punish you for all your iniquities" (Amos 3:2) as our sages expounded in Avoda Zara 4a. Otherwise [if one thinks G-d's kindness means He will overlook his sins], behold they said: "if a man says 'G-d will overlook my sins', his life will be overlooked", unless it is through [the system of] teshuva (repentance) and this is also a kindness.)

Another reason, is that good deeds are of two categories.

(1) Those concealed from others, and visible only to the Creator, like the duties of the heart, and other similar duties.

(2) Those visible in the limbs and not concealed from other creatures.

For the fulfillment of the visible duties of the limbs, the Creator rewards with visible reward of this world. While for fulfillment of concealed duties, He rewards with hidden reward, namely, in Olam Haba. Therefore, King David, spoke of this with words which hint to this matter, as written *"how great is Your goodness which You hid away for those that fear You; [which you have done for them that take refuge in You before the sons of men]"* (Tehilim 31:20). And likewise, the way of punishments for hidden and revealed misdeeds, is similar to the way of reward.

(*Pas Lechem*: The above verse mentioned "fear" which is concealed in the heart of a person, and ascribed to it concealed reward [in future tense]. Afterwards, the verse continues that those who "take refuge" in Him, i.e. who cling to Him in acts which are visible before the eyes of "the sons of men", and on these G-d already payed the reward. Hence, "which you have done" is in past tense.)

The proof for this view is as follows. G-d has guaranteed to His people that for their visible service, He would give them visible and swift reward in this world. This is explained in parsha *Bechukosai* "If you will go in My ways.." (Vayikra 26), and likewise, for visible sins, visible and swift punishment in this world. This is because the masses understand only that which is visible (tangible), not that which is hidden - as written: *"the hidden things belong to G-d, but the revealed things belong to us and to our children, forever"* (Devarim 29:28). And the verse says *"if the people will turn their eyes away from the [evil] acts of this man and his family, I will turn My face (send punishment) to this man and his family"* (Vayikra 20:4). Hence, the reward and punishment for the fulfillment or transgression of the duties of the heart belongs to the Creator. Therefore, Scripture omitted an explanation of their reward and punishment in the next world. (see Tov Halevanon for more details)

Another reason why rewards and punishments mentioned in scripture are limited to those in this world only is because the prophet is addressing worldly people. On the other hand, since Yehoshua (kohen gadol) was in the mystical world of angels (i.e. his soul was divested of his body at that time and was in the spiritual world - *PL*), G-d told him, *"I will give you a place to walk among these (angels) that stand"* (Zecharia 3:7). The proper way of motivating with hope and fear should be in accord with the time and place. Understand this.

(*Marpe Lenefesh*: During the giving of the torah at Sinai, the Jewish people were in this world. Hence it is proper to inform them of the reward and punishments of this world, since a man does not fear that which is not tangible to him and that he does not understand.

Tov Halevanon: "the prophet is addressing worldly people" means according to their attachment to physicality and physical pleasures which their hearts constantly turn to and seek the good of their bodies and fear what is harmful to it, while the spiritual pleasure or pain which their soul will be subject to in the next world is worth nothing to them compared to the physical pleasure or pain [in this world]. This is like in the Kuzari 1:104 ..... Therefore, G-d mentioned the rewards and punishments in this world according to what they hope for, and fear from, while they are alive here, namely, while they are attached to the physicality of the body and standing in this lowly world. But Yehoshua Kohen Gadol was an exceedingly wise man, pure, and already divested of the desires of physicality and he elevated himself to the level of the spiritual. For him, the main reward was spiritual pleasure and he desired it even while still in this world, as explained in the wisdom of truth (Kabala). For this he wrote "Understand this". [i.e. the plain meaning as in Marpe Lenefesh, and the deeper meaning here. Both are correct.])

Another reason is that the purpose of reward in Olam Haba is essentially clinging to G-d, and drawing near to His supernal light, as written *"your righteousness will go before you, the glory of G-d shall gather you in"* (Isaiah 58:8), and *"the wise will shine like the radiance of the firmament"* (Daniel 12:3), and also, *"To bring back his soul from the pit (i.e. Gehinom see below Tov Halevanon), to be enlightened with the light of the living"* (Job 33:30). And no one can reach there except he who the Creator finds favor in, and the favor of the Creator is the root of the reward, as written *"his anger is but a moment, in His favor is life"* (Tehilim 30:6). And there are hints in Parsha Bechukosai that pleasing the Al-mighty [is the greatest reward], this is what is written *"My soul will not abhor you"* (Vayikra 26:11), and *"I will turn to you and be unto you a G-d and you will be unto Me a people"* (ibid, 26:9).

(*Tov Halevanon*: "the purpose of reward" - The intent of this answer is that the spiritual reward is only clinging with G-d, and we will attain this when we minimize tending towards the bodily desires and purify our souls by fulfilling His commandments, blessed be He. And then, our souls will be fitting and capable of clinging to the spirituality of G-d. And then G-d, in His kindness, will "conceal us in the shadow of His hand" (Isaiah 49:2), even though we are not deserving of this reward from [the merit] of our deeds, but rather by "His kindness which prevailed over us" (Tehilim 117:2). But when a man turns towards the physical desires in rebelling against the Divine wisdom, then his soul is stuck in the darkness of the physical, and it is impossible in any way to draw close to Him, blessed be He, except by its cleansing itself from its tuma (spiritual impurity), in purifying itself from its physicality in Gehinom, as known to the sages. And according to this, reward and punishment in Olam Haba is not according to judgment and justice, like the reward and punishment in this world. Rather, they follow (1) a kind of nature (i.e. purity from the bad effects of physicality) and (2) also a desire of G-d for those who fulfill His will, both of these two things simultaneously. This is the difference between this answer and the previous one "a man does not become worthy of the reward of Olam Haba due to his good deeds alone... but rather it is a kindness..." [previous answer focused only on (2)]. Understand this.)

TRUST IN THE REWARD AND PUNISHMENT

Trusting in G-d regarding the reward in this world and in the next, which He promised to the righteous man for his service, namely, that He will pay reward to one who is fitting for it, and mete out punishment to one who deserves it. This is incumbent on the believer, and is an essential part of perfect faith in G-d, as written, "and he believed G-d, and it was counted to him as a righteousness" (Bereishit 15:6), and "had I not believed to see the goodness of G-d in the land of the living" (Tehilim 27:13).

(*Tov Halevanon*: "that He will pay reward to one who is **fitting** for it" - One who has perfected his soul by purifying its physical and has become fitting to draw near to the spiritual light should trust that G-d will desire in Him, and will draw His kindness on him in the reward of Olam Haba, even though he does not deserve it due to his deeds.
"and mete out punishment to one who **deserves** it" - i.e. punishment comes on him through the aspect of justice and is a debt which he became obligated in [and must pay].)

It is not proper for one to trust in his own good deeds, and assure himself that he will receive reward in this world and the next due to his good deeds. Rather, he should strive and exert himself [to do good] and make efforts to thank G-d and be grateful for His constant kindnesses to him, and not be motivated by hope of future reward for his deeds. Rather he should trust in G-d and try his best to pay his debt of gratitude for His great favors towards him, as our sages have said *"Do not be like servants who serve their master on condition of receiving reward. Rather, be like servants who serve their master without the condition of receiving reward, and let the fear of Heaven be upon you"* (Pirkei Avot 1:3).

(*Matanas Chelko*: This matter is subtle. Even though one must know that he will receive reward in the next world, nevertheless, the cause of doing the commandment should not be the receiving of the reward. Rather, one should do them because G-d commanded it and even if one did not receive any reward, he would do them anyways. He does the truth because it is the truth... Only that in this knowledge that he will receive reward, he rejoices more in fulfilling the will of G-d. (see there for more)

Tov Halevanon: "and let the fear of Heaven be upon you" - i.e. don't think that just like reward in the next world goes only by the grace and desire of G-d, so too the punishments of Olam Haba are not according to his deeds but only according to the desire of G-d... On this he wrote: "and let the fear of Heaven be upon you", i.e. the fear of punishment from above should nevertheless be upon you since punishment is according to Din (justice) in this world and in the next - not from the aspect of "desire".

Translator: Nevertheless, the Ramchal explains that even punishment is rooted in kindness, since the whole purpose of punishment is not as a revenge but rather in order to be able to bestow the greatest good on the person afterwards. G-d wants that the good a person receives in the afterlife is earned by him for this is the greatest good. If it were merely a free gift, then it would carry with it shame and would not be the greatest good. Thus the attribute of justice was created to ensure this good is earned and that the person's evil has a way of becoming pardoned.

Thus the attribute of justice does not have its own independent purpose. Rather, it is merely a method of bringing out G-d's conduct of love to actuality. Here is a quote from the Ramchal's book Daat Tevunot (siman 154):

"the second examination through which we study the ways of divine love is that through it itself stems the justice in all its general orders, namely, kindness, justice, and mercy (Chesed, Din, v'Rachamim)". End quote.

Likewise in Siman 138 there: "thus the mussar (sufferings) stems from actual love. Hence, a revealed rebuke stems from hidden love. Two good results come from this fundamental principle: 1) the mussar itself, even at the time when it is meted out, is not done with furious cruelty, but with great "sweetening" (mituk gadol) due to the hidden love which does not allow the anger to rule and become cruel". End quote.

Likewise the Ramchal writes in Kalach Pitchei Chachma, petach #2:
The desire of the Creator is only [to bestow] good. It is impossible to say that the Divine will desired that there could be other forces which can prevent Him [from bestowing good] in any manner whatsoever. Because the Divine will wants solely and exclusively to bestow good, [and if it were the case that other forces could prevent this] then it would certainly not be good that His goodness not be capable of spreading over His creations.

And if you ask: "[Perhaps] this is good, namely, the bestowing of good to the righteous and the punishing of the wicked [is good]?"

Behold, it is written: "I will have mercy upon whom I will have mercy" (Shemot/Exodus 33:19), [which was expounded to mean:] "even though he does not deserve it" (Berachot 7a), and it is written: "[In those days, and in that time, says the L-ord,] the iniquity of Israel shall be sought for, and there shall be none; [and the sins of Judah, and they shall not be found: for I will pardon them whom I preserve]" - behold G-d desires to bestow good also to the wicked.

Perhaps you will ask: "But all this is only after the long exile and the receiving of their punishments?".

I will answer you: "on the contrary, this is a support. If so, behold, the Divine will coordinates the matters so that in the end, all will be meritorious (see Derech H-shem part 2 ch.2-4). This demonstrates that the Divine will is truly and solely to bestow good, only that it is necessary to go with each person according to his way. For the wicked it is necessary to punish them in order to pardon them afterwards. If the intent [in punishing the wicked] was to expel them, then they should have been completely banished - not that they be punished in order to make them meritorious afterwards. This is a clear proof, because behold the end of a matter reveals the intended purpose of all the parts of that matter. And the end of the matter for every human being, whether the righteous or the wicked [after they are rectified] is to bestow on them good. If so, the intended purpose is to bestow good on all. Hence, the Divine will is solely good. Therefore, nothing will endure except His good.

Now that we have reached this point, namely, that the Divine will is only to bestow good, it is necessary that the matters do not go on like this indefinitely. Explanation: if the Divine will did not abhor destroying the wicked, then we would say that punishment is not something evil, rather "Evil pursues sinners" (Mishlei 13:21), and this is the way it is. But since we have said that the way is not like this, but rather, it [the punishment] is in order to afterwards bestow good on him, if so the punishment is evil and must be temporary, not eternal so that the sinner can be released from it. And since it is evil - it is against the Divine will. However, since it is against the Divine will, just like for each person, it is impossible for it to be eternal, so too for the world in general it is impossible for the existence [of evil] to be eternal. (just like G-d wants to rectify every wicked person, so too He wants to rectify the entire world, and nullify the existence of evil. But He wants man to have a hand in this in the meantime..)...

Now let us see if punishment, which precedes the [good] end for the wicked is [in actuality] good or not. A thing whose final end is different than its beginning - its beginning and end are not of the same kind. The process which will act on the wicked will be different in the end from what it was in the beginning. If so, the beginning of this process and the end of it are not of the same kind. The end is good, and this was what the active [Divine] will wanted in the beginning. The means, i.e. that which is before the end is not of this kind. If so, then what preceded the end is not good, and was not the desire of the active will.

We will answer this: If so, why did it change? Rather, since it is impossible to reach the end without this. But if it were possible without this, it would not be proper for this means to exist. The summary of all this is that punishment is evil, and it is the opposite of the desire and intent of the Divine will, but its existence is necessary to be created in order to reach from it to the ultimate purpose. If it were possible without this, it would have been deemed better by the Divine will... [see there for more])

One of the pious said "if one takes strict account of what he is obligated to the Creator for His kindness to him, no man would ever be worthy of the reward of Olam Haba for his deeds. Rather it is only as a kindness of the Al-mighty, therefore do not trust in your deeds." And King David said of this: *"to You, G-d, is kindness, for You pay a man according to his deeds"* (Tehilim 62:13) (i.e. even the paying of a man for his deeds is only a kindness)

SEVENTH CATEGORY - trust in G-d for the special grace to His treasured ones

The seventh category - trust in regard to G-d's special grace to His elect and treasured ones on whom many favors which are indescribable will be bestowed upon in Olam Haba. The proper way of trust in G-d is as follows: To exert oneself in the means which bring one to the high levels of the pious who are worthy of this special grace from G-d. This entails conducting oneself in the ways of the ascetics who loath worldly pleasures, and to uproot from one's heart the love of them and desire for them and replace these with the love of the Creator, and to devote oneself to Him, to delight in Him, to be desolate/astonished from the world and its inhabitants (see commentary), and to follow the ways of the prophets and the pious, and to trust that the Almighty will show him favor as He will do with them in the afterlife.

(*Tov Halevanon*: To transform the love of this world and its great longing, which is the way of people to long greatly for matters of this world and its pleasures, and transform it with the love of G-d in this way of love [i.e. not to extinguish the normal great love of this world and its superfluous things, but rather to channel this love to the love of G-d].

Matanas Chelko: ...without a doubt, we are talking here about a very lofty spiritual level. Nevertheless, we must understand that whenever a man loves someone or something, it is impossible for him to have perfect and complete love of G-d and of Olam Haba. This is the author's intent here. If one does not loath this world, he cannot love G-d at this level. Likewise, if one has love for worldly pleasures and matters in his heart he cannot love Olam Haba perfectly. Therefore, to reach this level, it is necessary to remove all love of this world from his heart and to loathe it.

Marpe Lenefesh: "to be desolate from the world and its inhabitants" - to not have any contentment in joining in the company of people, rather to distance from their conversations and social gatherings. (see gate #8)

Pas Lechem: that the remembrance of the affairs of this world and the ways of its inhabitants be desolate and absent from his heart. Or, the intent is that one is astonished and wonders in his heart from the world and its inhabitants, how they busy themselves without a [true] purpose, and "follow the vanities, etc." (Melachim II 17:15) and to abhor their affairs, as in "I was appalled by the vision; it was beyond understanding" (Daniel 8:27).

Matanas Chelko: i.e. that he has no contentment or pleasure from this world or its inhabitants
"to trust G-d will show him favor in the afterlife" - "trust"

means to trust in the kindness of G-d. For according to strict justice, there is no place for trust... nevertheless, there is a distinction between trust in worldly matters and trust in matters of the hereafter. For matters of this world, one can trust that G-d will do him favors even if he does not engage in the means of a livelihood, [for special scholars] such as Rabbi Shimon bar Yochai. But for matters of the next world it is impossible to trust in this manner. Because if one does not toil and do, if he does not love the next world and make it primary, but instead his love and desires are of this world, he cannot trust that G-d will grant the [bliss of the] afterlife to him as a kindness. It is impossible to attain the afterlife without hishtadlus (exertion). Only by exertion and strain in doing the will of G-d can one trust that he will receive good reward from the Creator in the afterlife. But without this, it is not trust but folly. This is what the author continues...

But one who trusts that G-d will thus favor him without the means of performing good deeds is a fool and a simpleton. He is like those of whom it is said "they act like Zimri and expect the reward of Pinchas" (Sota 22b). Some signs of those who have reached this high level are those who: (1) teach servants of G-d on the service (due to the love of G-d in all their being, they cannot hold themselves back from remaining silent on the falling short in the service of G-d in other people - *TL*), (2) demonstrating patient bearing and accepting in times of trial and difficulty, (3) regarding everything else as insignificant compared with the fulfillment of the commandments of G-d, as we see by the test of Avraham (Bereishit 22:1), or of Chananya, Mishael, and Azarya who were thrown in the fiery furnace (Daniel 3:13), or Daniel who was thrown in the lion's den (Daniel 6:13), or the 10 martyrs.

WHO IS WORTHY OF THE BLISS OF THE AFTERLIFE

Whoever chooses to die in the service of G-d, rather than rebel against Him; whoever chooses poverty rather than riches, sickness rather than health, suffering rather than tranquility, submits to the Creator's judgment, and desires in His decrees - such a person is worthy of the Divine grace of the Creator in the bliss of Olam Haba, of which it is written: *"That I may cause those that love Me to inherit substance; and I will fill their treasures"* (Mishlei 8:21), and *"no eye has ever seen, O G-d, beside You, what He has prepared for he that waits for Him"* (Isaiah 64:3), and *"How great is Your goodness that You have hidden away for those who fear You"* (Tehilim 31:20).

> (*Marpe Lenefesh*: The reason is that every mitzvah is not worthy of reward, as he wrote earlier in the sixth category, because as our sages said on: "Who has given Me anything beforehand, that I should repay him?" (Job 41:3) that first G-d bestowed all good to a person and afterwards man performs commandments to make a return. But one who offers his life and soul, and all that is his for G-d, out of love, then all the good of this world is worth nothing to him compared to his love of G-d. If so, how could he not be worthy of the good reward of the righteous and the just? This is clear.
>
> *Translator*: i.e. one who does not live for himself, but rather is "working" for G-d, then all the favors G-d does for him are "on the house" and in fact, even his mundane activities are considered as religious service as explained in Gate 3 chapter 9. See that entire gate at length with the commentaries for essential reading on properly understanding this gate.)

*** **Chapter 5** ***

The differences between one who trusts in G-d and one who does not with regard to employing the means for earning a livelihood, I say, are seven:

> (*Marpe Lenefesh*: i.e. both are engaged in the means, whether in a handicraft or in a business, and even so, there is a big difference between them)

(1) One who trusts G-d accepts His judgment in all his matters, and thanks Him for good as well as for bad, as written: *"G-d gave, G-d took back, blessed be His Name"* (Job 1:21), and as written: *"of kindness and of judgment I will sing to You"* (Tehilim 101:1), which the sages explained: *"if kindness, I will sing, if justice I will sing"* (Berachos 60b) (Rashi: when You bestow kindness upon me, I will praise you [with the blessing:] "Blessed be He Who is good and does good", and when You perform judgment upon me, I will sing, "Blessed be the true Judge." In either case, to You, O Lord, I shall sing), and they also said: "a man is under duty to bless G-d on the bad (with joy - *ML*) just like he blesses on the good" (Berachos 54a).

But one who does not trust in the Al-mighty boasts on the good (saying "it is due to my might and ingenuity, etc" - *PL*) as written "For the wicked boasts of his heart's desire" (Tehilim 10:3), and he becomes angry on the bad as written "And the one who passes therein shall suffer hardships and hunger, and it shall come to pass,] that when he shall be hungry, he shall be enraged, and curse his king and his [idolatrous] god, and he will turn to Heaven" (Isaiah 8:21).

> (*Marpe Lenefesh*: He will curse them since he sees they are of no substance (ein bo mamash).
> Rashi: *"And the one who passes therein"* - in abandoning the Holy One, blessed be He and relying upon the kings of the nations.
> *"and he will turn to Heaven"*: to beseech the Holy One, blessed be He, but G-d will not heed, for the verdict will have been sealed.

Matanas Chelko: one who trusts in G-d realizes that the results of all his efforts are only according to the will of G-d. Therefore, he thanks G-d whether he succeeds or not... but one who does not trust thinks that the exertion causes the success. And when he is not successful, he becomes angry at G-d or has some claims against Him [for not helping him]. In truth this is very strange, for if he has claims against G-d, then he recognizes that it is all from Him. Therefore, when he is successful why does he attribute this to his own strength and ingenuity? Why does he not also question G-d as to why he received such success?.. the answer is that he feels he is deserving of this success and is worthy of it. Only when bad things happen does he start to wonder what he did to deserve such bad things [why did G-d not help him] and he feels he did nothing wrong. All this stems from lack of trust. But one who trusts also wonders when he receives a great good that perhaps he does not deserve this, etc.)

(2) One who trusts in the Al-mighty has tranquility of spirit and a heart at ease regarding bad decrees, knowing that the Creator will arrange them for what is his good in this world and the next, as King David said *"my soul, wait you only on G-d; for my expectation is from Him"* (Tehilim 62:6). But one who does not trust in G-d, even when he is prosperous, is always pained and in a state of continual anxiety. He is saddened and grieving, because he is little satisfied with his situation, and yearns to augment, increase, and hoard in. And likewise in bad times because he is disgusted by it, and it is contrary to his desires, nature and traits. So too, the wise man said *"all the days of the poor are evil"* (Mishlei 15:15)

(*Matanas Chelko*: i.e. even if it is not good for him in this world, he knows and believes that it will be good for him in the next world. Therefore, he is not at all worried.

Tov Halevanon: *"all the days of the poor are evil"* - "poor" refers to one who is not content with what he has, as the sages said: "who is wealthy? One who is content with his portion." (Pirkei Avot)

Pas Lechem: *"yearns to augment, increase, and hoard in"* - corresponding to these three terms, he earlier wrote three terms denoting pain, namely:

(1) *"he is always pained"* - to **augment**. corresponding to love of pleasure, that whenever he is enjoying something, he is "pained" for augmenting the enjoyment from that thing.

(2) *state of continual anxiety* - to **increase**. corresponding to love of beneficial things, namely, money and possessions, he will "worry" always to increase his money

(3) *"saddened and grieving"* - to **hoard** in. corresponding to what he already possesses but which is spread out here and there and causes him mental distraction, he will be mourning to hoard it in. Likewise what his land produces and is outside in his field, he is saddened in that it is not assured from damages until he can bring it to his domain.

All this is during the times of prosperity. But during bad times, he is very pained and disturbed, *"because he is disgusted by it"* - corresponding to his taava (love of pleasure), whereby a person is disturbed and repulsed by the matter, either:

(1) because of absence of luxuries, and on this he wrote: "it is contrary to his desires", or

(2) because of absence of necessary things, and this subdivides into two general categories:

(a) "nature": That the matter disturbs his nature. For example, one who is of cold nature (i.e. he needs to stay cool), he is disturbed by bearing things which are too warm or vice versa.

(b) "traits": That the matter disturbs his traits. For example, one who is hot-tempered is irritated by those who act brazenly against him. And the opposite, one who is of calm nature, is irritated by the company of the hot-tempered.

So too, the wise man said "all the days of the poor are evil": that one who is not a baal bitachon (firmly trusts in G-d), is always poor in his mind, as above)

(3) One who trusts in G-d, even while he is engaging in the means for earning a livelihood, his heart will not rely on the means. And he will not hope to receive profit or loss from them unless it is the will of G-d. Rather, he engages in them as part of his service of G-d who commanded us to occupy ourselves with

the world, to maintain it and make it more habitable. If these means will yield him profit or help him avoid a loss, he will thank G-d alone for this, and he will not love and cherish the means more for this, nor will he rely more on them on account of this. Rather, his trust in G-d will be strengthened, and he will come to rely on Him and not the means. And if the means do not yield any benefit, he knows that his livelihood will come to him when G-d wants, and through whatever way He wants. Therefore, he will not reject the means because of this, nor abandon employing them, and thus he will serve his Creator (as above - *TL*).

But one who does not trust in G-d, engages in certain means because he places his trust in them, confident that they will yield him a profit and protect him against a loss. If they yield a profit, he will praise them and himself for his exertion in them and choosing them, and he will not try other means. But if they do not yield him a profit, he will abandon them and reject them, and lose interest in them, as written "Therefore he sacrifices to his net (through which he succeeded in his actions - *TL*), and he burns incense to his trawl, for through them he lives in luxury and enjoys the choicest food" (Chavakuk 1:16).

(*Matanas Chelko*: besides that he has no peace of mind in everything he does, he must also constantly change the means and strategies from one task or job to another. Through this he causes himself mental dispersion contrary to the peace of mind and tranquility of the one who trusts.

(4) One who trusts in G-d, if he has more money than he needs, he will spend it in a way which pleases the Creator (charity, etc.) with a generous spirit and a good heart, as written *"everything is Yours, and from Your hand we have given to You"* (Divrei Hayamim I 29:14). (since he knows and understands that everything is from G-d, and he is giving G-d of His money, certainly he will give with a generous spirit and a good heart - *PL*)

But one who does not trust in G-d, does not regard the entire world and everything in it as enough for his maintenance and sufficient for his needs. He is more concerned with saving his money than fulfilling his obligations to the Creator and to his fellow men, and he won't feel anything (of the causes which will suddenly strike his money - *PL*), until all of his money is lost and he is left destitute, as the wise man said: *"There is one that scatters, and yet increases; and there is one that withholds more than is right, but it leads to poverty"* (Mishlei 11:24).

(*Pas Lechem*: the intent of the verse is that even though both extremes are bad, because even excessive scattering (donating) is not proper, as the sages said in Ketuvot 50a, since sometimes one will become poor through this. Nevertheless, some do not become poor [by excessive donating], on the contrary he will increase from what he had, but "one that withholds more than is right" this leads only to poverty.

Matanas Chelko: the truster does not hold on to the extra money which remains after he has purchased his needs so that if, G-d forbid, he does not have enough money in the future, he will be able to sustain himself with this money. Rather, he gives it to others and spends it generously in the will of G-d, such as for tzedaka, or maaser. He knows that in truth everything is His. It all comes from Him, and G-d is fully capable of providing for him in the future for all of his needs. [i.e. he does not save beyond what is reasonable]

(5) One who trusts in G-d engages in a means of livelihood, in order to also prepare provisions for his end, and needs for his appointed home (in the afterlife). Only a means of livelihood which is clear to him that it is safe for fulfilling his torah study and fulfilling his religious service will he engage in it. But a livelihood which will bring any loss of torah observance or mislead him to rebel against G-d, he will not engage in, so as not to bring on himself spiritual sickness instead of healing.

(*Pas Lechem*: *"to also prepare provisions for his end, and needs for his appointed home"* - the word "provisions" applies to what a man will use on a journey, as written (in the exodus from Egypt) "nor had they prepared any provisions for themselves" (Shmos 12:39), or "Prepare provision for yourselves, [for in another three days you will cross this

Jordan...]" (Joshua 1:11), and when the soul leaves this world until it reaches its place, it will need provisions, as Rabbi Ploni said (before dying) "the provisions are scanty and the road is long" (Kesuvos 67b). And when the soul arrives to its appointed place, it will be sustained there forever and ever with what it prepared here, and on this he wrote "needs for his appointed home")

But one who does not trust in the Al-mighty, trusts in the means, and relies on them, and he won't refrain himself from employing any of them. He will engage in good means as well as bad means (i.e. those permitted to him as well as those forbidden to him - TL), and he won't think about his final end, as the wise man said, *"the wise man fears and avoids evil"* (mishlei 14:16).

(*Matanas Chelko*: he is always mindful that all matters of this world are only means to reach in the future to the afterlife. Therefore, he is always thinking that he must prepare provisions for his afterlife.

Marpe Lenefesh: He will have provisions for the afterlife.

Translator: In his youth, the Novhardok Rabbi asked Rabbi Yisrael Salanter why he should learn torah, saying "but what will I live with?". To which Rabbi Yisrael countered: "but what will you die with?")

(6) The one who trusts in G-d is beloved by all classes of people, and they feel at ease with him, because they feel secure that he will not harm them, and their hearts are at peace with regard to him. They are not afraid of him that he will take their wives or their money (etc, as in the tenth commandment, do not covet your fellow's wife, etc - PL), and he also is not worried about them because he realizes that it is not in any created being's power or control to benefit or harm him. Therefore, he does not fear harm from them nor expects any benefit from them. And since he is assured from them and they are assured from him, he will love them and they will love him, as written: *"he who trusts in G-d will be surrounded by kindness"* (Tehilim 32:10).

But he who does not trust in G-d, has no [true] friend, because he is always coveting others, and jealous of them, and he thinks that any good that reaches others is a loss to him (as if it was in his hand and left from him to them - *PL*), and that their livelihood is taken from his own, and (1) any preventing of attaining his desires is caused by them, and that (2) others are capable of helping him to obtain his desires, and (3) if some harm comes to his money or his children, he will think they caused it, and (4) that they are capable of removing the harm and problems from him, and since his thinking is based on these principles he will [come to] despise them, slander them, curse them, and hate them. And he is the disgusting one in both worlds, regarded as a disgrace in both abodes as written: *"a crooked heart will not find good"* (Mishlei 17:20).

(*Pas Lechem*: He thinks *"any preventing of attaining his desires is caused by them"*, or he thinks that even though they did not cause him to be prevented from attaining his desires, but nevertheless, since it is in their ability to assist him to attain his desires and they don't assist him - he will hate them.

Pas Lechem: *"he will despise others, slander them, curse them, and hate them"* - He specified four types of denigration corresponding to these four previous divisions.
Corresponding to: (1) *"any preventing of attaining his desires is caused by them"*, he wrote: *"he will despise them"*.
Corresponding to: (2) that they don't want to assist him in attaining his desires, he wrote: *"slander them"*, since he is upset with them because of this and he speaks bad of them calling them midah sedom (selfish, refusing to help others), or the like.
Corresponding to: (3) *"if some harm comes to his money or his children, he will think they caused it"*, he wrote: *"he will curse them"*.
Corresponding to: (4) that they don't want to save him from his troubles, he wrote *"and hate them"*, since according to his view they hate him and rejoice on his troubles, therefore he also hates them.

Matanas Chelko: Trust is a foundation of all commandments

between man and his fellow man. For perfection in fulfilling these commandments and in the commandment of "love your fellow..." comes through trust in G-d. The reason a man is not so much able to love his fellow is because when he sees that he is not succeeding as much as his fellow, he imagines that this is due to his fellow. But the truster realizes that it is all from G-d and His decrees. Through this he can feel only love for each and every person.... As we brought earlier from the Sefer Hachinuch (mitzva 241) on the commandment of not exacting revenge which is based on trust that everything occurs solely through the will of G-d, see there. But with this thought (of trust) it is impossible for him to hate his fellow or have complaints against him. Likewise for jealousy. It cannot occur in one who trusts in G-d. Hence, all matters of commandments between man and his fellow are rooted in the trait of trust.

(7) The one who trusts in G-d will not mourn if his requests are denied, or if he loses something he loves, and he will not hoard possessions nor be troubled by more than his day's needs (see below commentaries). He does not worry about what will be tomorrow since he does not know when his end will come. He therefore trusts in G-d to prolong his days, and provide his sustenance and needs during this time. He neither rejoices nor grieves about the future (i.e. he does not rejoice in hoping for a future good which is coming up and likewise, he does not grieve or worry on any future bad thing coming up - *PL*), as written *"do not delight in tomorrow because you don't know what today could bring"* (Mishlei 27:1), and Ben Sira said "do not anguish about the troubles of tomorrow because one doesn't know what today could bring, perhaps tomorrow he will be no more (i.e. perhaps you will not live to see tomorrow - *ML*), and he had anguished on a world that is not his" (Sanhedrin 100b).

Rather, his worry and mourning is on his lackings in the fulfillment of his obligations to G-d, and he tries to make up as much as he can of them, of his external (actions - *PL*) and internal duties (of the heart - *PL*). For he thinks of his death and the arrival of the day of in-gathering, and the fear that death may come suddenly increases his efforts and zeal to prepare provisions for his end, and he won't be concerned about preparing for this world. This is what our sages said "repent one day before your death" (Avos 2:10). They explained on this (Shabbat 153a): "repent today, perhaps you will die tomorrow, therefore let all your days be in repentance, as written 'at all times let your clothing be clean' " (Koheles 9:8).

> (*Pas Lechem*: "*he thinks of his death and the arrival of the day of ingathering*" - "thinks of his death", the intent is on the death of the body and the nullification of his [worldly] desires. Thinking of "the arrival of the day of ingathering", the intent is on the ingathering of the soul to its place. Both contemplations are necessary because in remembering the death of the body, he will be repulsed by its desires, while by remembering the ingathering of the soul, he will worry on his sins, which prevent the ascent of the soul to its place.
>
> *Rabbi Yaakov Emden*: "*nor be troubled by more than his day's needs*" - i.e. he does not ask of G-d more than his day's needs, as written: "[give me neither poverty nor riches,] but give me only my daily bread" (Mishlei 30:8). He will not trouble himself much for that which is not already arranged for him. For example, if he rents out things or works at a handicraft he will not worry about whether he will find a renter or a buyer tomorrow. Rather, he will trust that G-d will provide his daily bread, as written: "[Behold, I will rain bread from heaven for you;] and the people shall go out and gather a certain portion every day" (Shmos 16:4). And our sages said: "he who has what to eat today and asks 'what will I eat tomorrow?' is of those who are little in faith" (Sotah 48b).
>
> However, one whose work is for a set duration and at a set period (of the year) such as farmers - certainly he must exert himself on the day and period (season of the year) which will be good for many days and for difficult times, as written: "he that gathers in summer is a wise son" (Mishlei 10:5), and he exhorted us to learn from the ant: "Go to the ant, you sluggard; consider her ways, and be wise...it stores its provisions in summer and gathers its food at harvest" (Mishlei 6:6), to learn from its ways and be wise to prepare

during times available. And likewise, one who engages in business must journey to markets and fairs or the like. There is no prohibition to fill storehouses and to rely on them for years of famine, or to save cattle and properties from the extra that G-d has made available to him, so that it be ready for the time of need, and thus it is written in the torah: "But you must remember the L-rd your G-d, for it is He that gives you strength to make valor" (Devarim 8:18), which the Onkelos renders: "He gives you counsel to acquire wealth", and the wise man said: "The wealth of the rich is the city of his strength; the destruction of the poor is their poverty" (Mishlei 10:15), when it is wealth that was earned justly - take care of it, and do not kick at the blessing of G-d. Also, one is not obligated to scatter it all [to tzedaka, etc.], but rather through certain conditions. The intelligent person will arrange his matters according to the way of nature in accord with the will of G-d who arranged for him an order to seek his livelihood at certain times, with a perfect and faithful heart that trusts in G-d.

Matanas Chelko: *"nor be troubled by more than his day's needs"* - there is no doubt that the author is speaking about very lofty levels of trust, really (mamash) the greatest possible extreme of the trait - that one does not worry about tomorrow. Nevertheless, reason also necessitates that it be such. For when one contemplates on what happened yesterday and further back, he will see that he always had what to live on and what to eat, and everything was only through G-d. Then too, he had nothing for tomorrow. Therefore, even today he can also rely on G-d for tomorrow. But the imagination deceives him and tells him that it is not comparable for in those past times he certainly had enough for the next day. But in truth, it is not so. Therefore, one needs to work on feeling this level of trust and live in this way.

"since he does not know when his end will come" - this is a different point. The truster is not a dreamer. On the surface it seems that the wicked is more assured than the truster. For behold, the truster always worries that perhaps he will die tomorrow, as Rabbi Eliezer told his disciples "repent today

for tomorrow you may die" (Shab.153a) But the wicked does not live by this idea. But in truth, it is not so (that the wicked is more assured). For the end of every human being is death. This is not a thought of sadness. On the contrary, it is proper and beneficial. A man should constantly contemplate that he is given a fixed amount of time to live and work in this world. But the wicked does not contemplate this thought "to repent for perhaps he will die tomorrow". Rather, he trusts that certainly tomorrow and the day after he will still be among the living. This is a bit amazing for most people see through television, or the like, many murders, and that people do die, but they don't take to heart that it is possible they will also die like them. Rather, whenever they start to think about their deaths, they fall into great sadness. They feel so assured that they will be alive tomorrow and the day after that they don't even worry about this. It is known what the Chafetz Chaim said on how a man goes to a funeral and sees that people die, but does not reflect that perhaps he will also die tomorrow. Rather, he thinks that just like there is a "chevra kadisha" (funeral worker group), so too there is a "chevra of the dead", and he is not part of this group and is not counted among them. In truth, this is just repressing of the eye. For one must reflect on the time of his end in this world. This is not a matter of sadness [to avoid] but rather like a farmer working on his field who still has much work to do. If his friend tells him to finish everything quickly before nightfall for then he will not be able to work, certainly he will not answer him: "don't speak to me about night, for it is sad and dark". Likewise for death, which is the time of nightfall for a man. Therefore, one must and is under duty to reflect on his time for work in this world.)

But one who does not trust in G-d, mourns greatly the constant troubles of the world that befall him, that his wishes and the things he loves are taken away or denied from him (he worries constantly that these things will be lacking to him - TL). He tries to amass much wealth of this world, as if he were assured from passing on (that his situation passes from this world to the next - TL), and the fear of death has left him, as if his days are unlimited and his life will never end. He does not consider his end, occupied only with this world, unconcerned about his religious matters, making no provisions for the hereafter, and his eternal abode. His trust in prolonging his days in this world is a cause for his perpetual desire for his worldly affairs and for his little desire in matters of his final end.

> (*Matanas Chelko*: *"his trust in prolonging his days..."* - in truth this is a great wonder. One who does not trust in G-d, trusts in only one thing - that he will not die and will live forever. For everything else he relies on his own strength and ingenuity, and that he has the power to decide and succeed. But regarding life and death, which everyone knows and recognizes that it is in G-d's hands - on this he trusts that he will live forever! This is what we wrote in the beginning of this gate, namely, that really every person trusts in something, and it is impossible to live otherwise. The difference is whether a person trusts in G-d, human beings, or in himself. For example, one who rides an airplane trusts in the mechanics that no failure will occur, and likewise on the pilot who knows how to drive the airplane. Likewise, he trusts that the baker did not put poison in the bread, and similarly for every thing. The reason is that this is the nature G-d implanted in man - to trust. For without this, it is impossible to live. One would be worried on every little thing, be it the baker or the workers, etc. [The proper way is that] in every thing it is proper to place one's trust in G-d (not the baker, etc.), but in things one does not know what will be, such as death, one must prepare for himself provisions for the journey.

When the preacher rebukes him or the teacher instructs him saying "how long will you avoid thinking about preparing provisions for your final journey and for matters of your eternal abode?"

He will answer "when I will have enough money for my needs and for the needs of my wife and children until the end of our days. Then I will have peace of mind from my worries of this world, and I will take time to pay my debts to the Creator, and will think about preparing provisions for my final end."

*** Chapter 6 ***

I saw proper to expose the foolishness and error in this way of thinking in 7 ways. I will reveal the greatness of their mistake, and if our words prolong, this is because there is much to shame and rebuke proponents of this outlook.

> (*Pas Lechem: "foolishness and error"* - Some of the matters he will bring demonstrate to the person that he is a complete fool, similar to one of the boorish people who have no human understanding. Other matters he will bring do not demonstrate his foolishness so much but rather show that he is mistaken, such as the fifth, sixth, and seventh.
>
> Afterwards, he wrote: "there is much to shame and rebuke..." corresponding to these two "foolishness and mistake", because a man is shamed when he is called a fool, and on the "mistake", he wrote "and rebuke", namely, to clarify his mistake to him.)

They are as "security pledge seekers", similar in their practice to merchants who sell goods on credit to someone he does not trust, and will demand a security pledge at the time of sale, because he minimally trusts his client or fears the client will not be able to pay him.

(1) The first of the possible ways to answer him: we tell him "You, the man who doubts the decree of the Creator, and doubts His [Almighty] power, you whose light of intellect has obscured, whose candle of understanding has extinguished due to being overwhelmed by the darkness of material desires. You deem proper to seek a security pledge from a client who has no dominion over you, and cannot give you orders. However, for a worker who seeks to be hired by an employer, it is not proper for him to seek a security pledge of his wages before he starts to work. All the more so, it is not proper for a slave to seek a security pledge of his food from his master before working for Him. And even more so, for a created being to seek a pledge from his Creator before fulfillment of the service he owes Him!

It is a wonder! For a slave to undertake service to his master with a precondition that the master pay him a wage after his service is completed would be regarded as a disgrace (since the owner boards, lodges, and clothes him and provides for all his needs - Rabbi Hyamson zt'l), as the sages said: *"be not like servants who serve their master on condition to receive reward, but rather like servants who serve their master even without condition of receiving reward"* (Pirkei Avot 1:3). And how much more so if he were so brazen as to demand a pledge for his maintenance from his master before he even starts working. On similar to this it is written: *"Is this how you repay the L-ord, you disgraceful, unwise people?! [Is He not your Father that has acquired you? has He not made you, and established you?]"* (Devarim 32:6).

> (*Pas Lechem*: *"who doubts the decree of the Creator"* - you are of those of little faith, who doubt the decree of the Creator, i.e. who doubt whether or not all of a man's guidance and needs are governed exclusively by the decree of the Creator.
>
> *"and doubts His [Almighty] power"* - you doubt His power, and the scope of His providence which spreads from the highest heavens (spiritual worlds) until the depths of our [physical] world, since the doubt on the providence [of G-d] in this world stems from their imagining and picturing the remoteness of the physical from His glorious holy place.
>
> *Marpe Lenefesh*: *"whose light of intellect has obscured, whose candle of understanding has extinguished due to being overpowered by the darkness of material desires"* - i.e. since the darkness of his material desires has overpowered him, therefore "the light of intellect has obscured, and the candle of understanding has extinguished", to the extent that he does not understand even self-evident things which no man is capable of denying.
>
> *Tov Halevanon*: *"even the work of a slave to a master on condition to be paid after the work is regarded as a disgrace"* - that which he does not know his owner (a reference to Isaiah 1:3 "The ox knows his owner...but Israel does not

know"), who acquired him with his money on condition that he serve him. And all the more so, the Holy One, blessed be He, who is our Father, He acquired us, and it is proper for us to serve Him on account of the multitude of favors He has already bestowed on us, as the author wrote in the previous chapter.)

(2) One who takes a security pledge from a client receives a definite amount and his request is limited. But for the proponent of this thinking, there is no end to what he seeks. For he does not know how much money will suffice for his and his family's needs and luxuries for the rest of their lives. And even if he obtained money many times his needs, he would not be at peace, because the time of their end is hidden, and the number of their days is not known, and he is foolish in what he seeks because there is no end by him and no measure.

> *Pas Lechem*: *"no end by him"* to the amount of his needs since he does not know how long he will live, and corresponding to the desire for luxuries, he wrote "no measure" since there is no measure for luxuries.
>
> *Translator*: since he does not know his end, he imagines and conducts his life as if he will live forever as The Zohar wrote (Nasso 126):"A man walks in this world and he thinks that it will be his forever, and that he will remain in it for all time" (i.e. even though he knows intellectually that he will die, but he does not feel this at all).

(3) One who takes a security pledge from his fellow, only does so if there are no previous debts that he owes the fellow, and the fellow has no claims against him. Only then is he justified to request a pledge. But if he has outstanding debts to the fellow, and knows the fellow has legitimate claims against him, he has no business whatsoever in seeking a pledge, and it is not proper for him to accept it even if the fellow volunteered the pledge.

All the more so, for the Creator who has such legitimate claims on man, so that if the service of all human beings who ever lived could be accumulated and credited to a single man, their total would not be sufficient return to cover the debt of gratitude that a man owes for even one of the benefits the Creator bestowed on him (such as bringing him to existence from nothingness).

> (*Pas Lechem*: This is because the intent in the word "return" is: the receiving of a favor that the benefactor receives in return from the one who he benefited. But for G-d, it is completely not applicable to render to Him any favor from His creations. Therefore, it cannot be considered a "return".
>
> *Matanas Chelko*: As written (Job 41:11) "Who has given Me anything beforehand, that I should repay him?", i.e. no man has ever done any commandment without having first received countless benefits from G-d. His life, possessions, and all matters - everything comes from G-d. The reason man cannot repay G-d is twofold. First, in truth, G-d does not get anything whatsoever from the fulfilling of His commandments. Hence, the fulfilling of a commandment cannot be considered a payment for all that one received. Secondly, all that a man does is worth less than a drop in the ocean in comparison with the gift of life which G-d has graced to man. All that man does - Shabbat, tefilin, talit, etc. is not payment for even one second of life.)

And how can this brazen faced person not be ashamed to ask from the Creator big favors on top of previous favors thereby increasing his debt to Him. (the man seeks from G-d more favors, and that they be bigger than the favors He bestowed on him until now - *PL*). And maybe he will not even be able to fulfill the service that he says he will do (after he acquires wealth) because his days will have passed and his end will have come.

> (*Pas Lechem*: "his days will have passed and his end will have come" - two expressions corresponding to two categories of a person's death. One, that the number of days allotted to him from the time of his birth have passed, as is known, that every person has a fixed number of days allotted to him. Two, due to a heavenly decree because of some sin for which he incurred a death sentence.)

One of the pious would say to people: "Gentlemen, is it conceivable that the Creator would demand payment today for debts that are not due until tomorrow? And likewise, would He demand payment today for debts that are not due until next year, or many years from now?"

They answered him, "How is it possible to claim from us payment of future debts when we don't even know if we will be living at the time when the debt is incurred? Rather, we are only bound to perform a definite service for a definite time and when the future comes, we will perform the service that is due then."

He would answer them: "So too, the Creator guarantees for you for every definite period its needed livelihood, and in return for this, you are indebted a great service (in that time period - PL). Just like He does not demand from you the special service before its appointed time, so too you should feel ashamed to ask for income before the time for it has arrived. Why do I see you seeking from Him income for several years in the future when you don't even know if you will live to reach those days? Furthermore, you ask Him to provide you with maintenance for a wife and children which you don't even have yet. You are not satisfied with the livelihood provided in the present and you seek to prepare money for needs and luxuries for future times that you are uncertain to reach and that are not assured to you. And, not only do you not render to Him service for the benefits you will receive in the future, but you don't even make an accounting with yourselves for the service to Him which you neglected to do in the past during which G-d has not neglected to provide for your livelihood in full."

(4) One who takes a security pledge from his fellow does so for one of three reasons: One, maybe the fellow will become poor and won't be able to pay him. Two, maybe the fellow will close his hand [refuse to pay] and he may be unable to collect payment from him. Three, in case the fellow dies or won't be found.

The security pledge is like a medicine against these ailments that occur between people (i.e. if he takes a pledge he is immune from these ailments and worries - TL). But if men were assured of each other against these three mishaps, it would certainly be disgraceful to demand a security pledge. And the Creator for whom these three mishaps do not apply, how much more so is it a great disgrace to demand a security pledge from Him. And scripture already says: *"silver and gold is Mine"* (Chagai 2:8), and *"wealth and honor belong to You"* (Divrei Hayamim 29:12).

(*Tov Halevanon*: It is not applicable to ask any kind of pledge from Him since everything is already by Him.

Pas Lechem: The latter two reasons do not need a proof [from scripture], because who is so foolish as to not know that He is living and among us, and that He has no trace of dishonesty or stinginess, ch'v. But on the first reason, perhaps a person will think "from where will G-d pay me, since He does not make coins?" On this he brought the verse "silver and gold is Mine", that nevertheless He has full capacity to give to whomever He wishes

Matanas Chelko: *"disgrace to demand a security pledge from Him"* - for G-d will not become poor or die. He can give whenever He wants. Only that a man doesn't believe in G-d and His ability. Therefore he seeks a pledge. But G-d already promised in His torah that human beings should do the commandments and He will support them all of their days.)

(5) One who obtains a security pledge from his fellow will be at peace with his pledge because he expects to collect from it and to derive benefit from it or its monetary value. But one who thinks that if the Creator will advance him future provisions he will have peace of mind regarding affairs of this world - his thinking is false and mistaken, because he cannot be sure the money will remain by him. It is possible that he will be struck by some mishap that parts him from the money, as written *"in mid-life he will lose it"* (Yirmiyahu 17:11).

And as for the claim that he will have peace of mind when he amasses wealth - this demonstrates falsehood and foolishness on his part. On the contrary this may well be the very cause that will cause him much mental pressure and anxiety as our sages said *"more possessions, more worries"* (Avot 2:7)..

(*Pas Lechem*: *"this demonstrates falsehood and foolishness"* - either he is mistaken in this, or he himself knows this and deceives with this excuse.

Marpe Lenefesh: Even though it is a mistake to demand a pledge from G-d for many reasons, nevertheless, if he were assured that the money (pledge) would stay by him and that he could do what he wants with it, his mistake would not be a falsehood. For example, suppose he took a pledge from someone who he did not realize that the man is an honorable and wealthy person. Even though he was mistaken in demanding a pledge, nevertheless, since he did not know the man, it is not falsehood, since nevertheless, he is assured by the pledge from many possible mishaps. But this that he took a pledge from G-d, not only was he mistaken in his outlook, but also his mistake will not yield any benefit. For he is still not assured that the money (pledge) will be by him at a needy time. Perhaps the money will be struck by a loss and nothing will remain or maybe he will die at midlife as [we see] happens every day. And even if we say that the wealth will stay by him, nevertheless it is uncertain whether he will serve G-d due to having wealth, because perhaps the money will bring him more mental pressure and anxiety than he had before he had it, since "more possessions, more worries")

(6) If one who takes a security pledge from his fellow were certain that the fellow would pay him before the due time, and would out of pure kindness compensate him with an amount twice as much as was due for his waiting time, he would not seek a security pledge under any circumstances. Now, the blessed Creator, of who it is known to us of His benevolent conduct towards us, and of His great past and present favors to us, and that He rewards acts of righteousness and service with reward that we cannot even imagine, as written: *"no eye had ever seen, O G-d, besides Yours, what He has prepared for those who wait (trust and hope - TL) to Him"* (Isaiah 64:3), certainly it is a great disgrace to ask for a security pledge.

(*Marpe Lenefesh:* *"reward that we cannot even imagine"* - that He bestows so much good reward for one mitzvah.
Pas Lechem: the hidden reward cannot be imagined by the human mind. All the more so, it cannot be described

| verbally.)

(7) One who takes a security pledge from his fellow, is only justified in doing so if he is able to supply him with the merchandise purchased for which he takes the pledge. But one who seeks a security pledge from the Creator, in seeking advance favors, is not capable of paying for them in services. He is not even certain of paying back what he owes from past debts, all the more so for paying what he owes for future favors. For the righteous man cannot pay back the debts of gratitude of the Al-mighty on him except through the means of help which G-d renders him. And so, one of the pious in his praises of G-d said: "Even the thinking person who has knowledge of You, does not praise his own religious acts, but rather praises Your Name and mercy, for You have prepared his heart to know You. Through You (Your help - *ML*) the people of Israel will be found worthy and be praised saying: *"We praised [ourselves] with G-d all day long, and we will forever thank Your Name"* (Tehilim 44:9).

(*Marpe Lenefesh*: For example, if the lender takes a security pledge on condition that he will lend the borrower a 1000 gold coins. Then, if the lender has the 1000 gold coins available, he can take the security pledge. If he does not [have the 1000 gold coins available], then he cannot take it. And a man knows that he does not have the ability to pay G-d in [religious] services and righteousness corresponding to all the benefits he gets from G-d. And especially, if he pays back a little bit, it is through G-d's help, as our sages expounded (Midrash Vayikra Rabba 27:2) on the verse: "Who has given Me anything beforehand, that I should repay him?" (Job 41:3) - Who put up a mezuzah before I gave him a house? [Who built a Sukkah before I gave him a place upon which to build it? Who performed the mitzvah of tzitzis before I gave him clothing?], likewise, even one's wisdom and praises is from Him, blessed be He.

Matanas Chelko: even when a man praises G-d, the recognition itself that man has of G-d is from G-d, and the mouth with which he utters the praises is from G-d. Everything he does is using the tools which G-d has given him. This is what we say in the "Aleinu Leshabeach" prayer: "it is incumbent on us to praise the Master of the world... [and concludes] that we bow and praise the King of kings". What kind of praise is it to say that our portion is to praise Him? Rather, it is the exact same thing the author is saying; we are praising G-d for giving us the permission, ability, and opportunity to praise Him. Likewise, in the Modim prayer, it starts "we thank You..." and ends "on our thanking you"... The point is that a man does not do any "kindness" towards G-d. On the contrary, the kindness is from G-d who gave us the ability and possibility to come to the synagogue and pray to Him and praise Him. If one reflects on this, he will see it is the exact opposite of the outlook of the pledge-seeker who wants to receive everything before the service. But in truth, all the service they do - it is all from G-d.

*** **Chapter 7** ***

Since we have completed in this gate, to the best of our ability, a fitting amount of discussion on the themes of trust, it is now proper to clarify the things detrimental to trust in the Al-mighty. I say that the detrimental things mentioned in the 3 preceding gates of this book are all likewise detrimental to trust [in G-d].

> (*Marpe Lenefesh*: i.e. the Unity - to believe in the Creator of the world, as explained there [in Gate #1], and likewise on the [Gate of] examination, to examine His creations, and to assume the service of the Creator, as is fitting to Him. Whoever is far from the things mentioned in those gates and fell into the things detrimental to them as was explained earlier - he undoubtedly does not trust in G-d.
>
> *Pas Lechem*: (from the introduction) On the other things of the inner duties such as placing one's trust in G-d, giving over oneself to Him, and devoting one's acts to Him, and the like, which stem from recognizing the greatness of G-d and of His beneficence.)

Additional things which cause a loss of trust:
(1) Ignorance with regard to the Creator and His good attributes. For one who does not realize the Creator's mercy towards His creations, His guidance, providence and rule over them, and that they are bound by His chains, under His total control - he will not be at peace (from mishaps - *PL*) and will not rely on Him (for providing his needs - *PL*).

> (*Marpe Lenefesh*: *"Ignorance with regard to the Creator"* - he does not realize that G-d is a great and awesome King and that His reign is over everything.
> *"and His good traits"* - how He guides His creations with kindness and mercy, and always gives them all their needs.
> *"that they are bound by His chains"* - all the creations are truly bound by Him, that everything is from Him, all things that a human being does is completely from Him, and there is nobody who can change anything, except for Yirat Shamayim (fear of G-d, i.e. moral choice) which G-d gave the free will in man's hands.

Pas Lechem: (from the introduction) On the other things of the innner duties such as placing one's trust in G-d, giving over oneself to Him, and the like, *which stem from recognizing the greatness of G-d and of His beneficence.*)

(2) Another, ignorance of the Creator's commandments, namely His Torah, where He instructed us in it to rely on Him and trust in Him, as written: *"test Me in this..."* (Malachi 3:10), and *"trust in G-d forever"* (Isaiah 26:4).

(*Tov Halevanon*: *"to rely on Him and trust in Him"* - in [performing] His service and guarding His commandments, and like our sages expounded: "take maaser so that you become rich", and [G-d] says: "test Me in this", i.e. in maaser, and likewise for all of the other mitzvot, and like the verse says (Tehilim 37:25): "yet I have not seen the righteous forsaken")

Another detriment to trust is to tend to rely on the means which one can see, without realizing that the nearer the causes are to the one affected by them, the less ability they have to help or harm him, and the further [up] they are, the stronger and the more power it has to help or harm him.

As an illustration, when a king decides to punish one of his servants, he commands his prime minister to take care of it, and the prime minister orders his chief of police, and the chief of police orders his sergeant, and the sergeant orders his officer, and the officer orders the policeman, and the policeman inflicts the punishment with the instruments (whip, stick, etc.) he has.

The instruments have the least capability of all of them to reduce or increase his suffering because they have no will of their own. The policeman has greater capability than the instruments (to reduce the number of whippings - PL). Likewise, the officer has greater capability than the policeman, and the sergeant than the officer, and the chief of police than the sergeant, and the prime minister than the chief of police, and the king more than all of them, because if he wants, he can pardon the man (from everything - TL).

As you can see, the weakness and strength of the agents to affect the person are according to their remoteness from him or nearness to him. And the exalted Creator, who is the First Cause and infinitely remote from those affected by Him, is the One who it is proper to trust and rely on because of His infinite power to help or harm, as we explained.

> (*Marpe Lenefesh*: the thing near to him from which his livelihood comes has less power to provide his livelihood than the thing remote from him, which is the cause of this [near] thing, and this remote thing to another more remote thing, etc. All these agents from the man on are called causes and means, and G-d is the Means of all the means and the Cause of all the causes, and the man who receives from all the means is called "the affected". Understand this.)

The general principle in the matter of trust is that the degree of trust among those who trust in G-d increases according to the amount of knowledge of G-d, faith in His protection of them, and in His abundant providence to promote what is for their good.

> (*Tov Halevanon*: "increases according to the amount of knowledge of G-d" - knowing and understanding the extent of His reign on each and every act and cause - that everything depends on Him, blessed be He. He will now bring an analogy to explain the matter.
>
> *Pas Lechem*: The degree of level of trust among people, namely, the degree of trust which people differ in is "according to the amount of knowledge of G-d, etc."
>
> *Marpe Lenefesh*: The proof of this is what he will mention shortly, that a baby at first trusts in his mother's breast, and afterwards on his mother, and afterwards on his father, and so on for the 10 levels he mentions. From this it is clear that the greater one's knowledge of G-d and of His providence on him, the more trust in G-d he will have.)

THE TEN LEVELS OF TRUST
(1) An infant, at the beginning of his existence, trusts in his

mother's breast, as written: *"For You drew me from the womb; You made me trust on my mother's breasts"* (Tehilim 22:10).

> (*Matanas Chelko*: i.e. if the baby could speak and one would ask it how it lives, it would respond "from my mother's breast", not "from my mother". In his eyes, the breast feeds and sustains him. This is the outlook of a baby. He cannot grasp more than this.

(2) When his perception strengthens, his trust moves to his mother, due to the great care she gives him, as written: *"I swear that I calmed and quieted my soul like a weaned child with his mother"* (Tehilim 131:2).

> (*Matanas Chelko*: when he grows a bit and his intellect opens a bit more, he recognizes that he receives several benefits from his mother, such as washing him, clothing him, etc. Hence, now he realizes that his sustenance comes from his mother. It is proper to add here the following analogy from the trust of a child to his mother and father. When a child stands on a table or chair and his father asks him to jump to his hands and the child does so. Certainly, without strong trust in his father, that his father worries for him and loves him, he would never have jumped thereby placing himself in danger of falling to the floor. His trust in his father is so great that he jumps to his hands. Likewise, for a man's trust in G-d, he must jump into the hands of G-d and trust in Him that He cares for him and loves him just like a father's love for his child.

(3) When his understanding grows more, and he observes that his mother depends on his father, he moves his trust to his father due to the greater degree of protection he receives from him.

> (*Tov Halevanon*: the security and food which she bestows on him - everything depends on the gift from the hand of the father.
>
> *Marpe Lenefesh*: Even though his mother takes care of his needs, and not his father since he is not available, nevertheless, he recognizes his father's protection, that

sometimes his father saves him from things which cause him pain.)

(4) When his body strengthens, and it becomes possible for him to earn for himself a livelihood through work or business, or the like, he moves his trust to his strength and resourcefulness, due to his ignorance that all the good that came before this was through the providence of G-d.

(*Tov Halevanon*: he is still boorish and does not realize that wealth does not come from the trade itself, and all the livelihood he received until now was from G-d.)

It is said of one of the pious, whose neighbor was a swift scribe and would earn his livelihood through his scribal skills. One day he inquired to the scribe: "how are things?" He answered "good, as long as my hand is still in good shape." Then, that evening his hand was crushed, and he could not write with it for the rest of his life. This was his punishment from G-d, in that he placed his trust in his hand. (to atone for him. Note that he must have been at a very high level of piety, therefore G-d paid him in this world even for minute sins so as to spare him from any loss in the next world)

(*Matanas Chelko*: "as long as my hand is still in good shape" - certainly it is permitted to speak like this. However, it all depends on one's intent. If he means "thank G-d, I still have the hand given to me to do my work", that he understands that the strength does not come from himself. Rather it is given to him by the grace of G-d, then his words are good and correct. However, it appears that the author's intent is that even words like this ascribe too much the ability and accomplishment to human power. If he thinks this is the way to his livelihood, that by G-d's giving him a hand, he is able to use it to work and earn a livelihood for himself, this is already considered shituf (association), G-d and himself. Since, what comes out of his words is that his intent is if he did not have a hand, he would not be able to provide for himself. This is not correct. For G-d can provide for him through other means. True, right now G-d gave him a hand through which he is providing for himself, but true trust is to recognize that even without his hand, G-d can still provide for him through his feet, his head or any other way. Hence, whenever a person ascribes excessive power and ability in the means itself, he already diminishes thereby his trust in G-d.

Netziv commentary on Gen.40:23 - G-d punished Yosef for putting his trust in the Wine Master by causing the Wine Master to forget about Yosef for two years (Midrash, Genesis Rabba 89:3). From the fact that Yosef was punished for putting his trust in a person we learn about his greatness. The punishment indicates that Yosef had never before put his trust in man and was thus punished solely because he deviated from his high level of trust in G-d.

(5) If his livelihood comes through one of his fellow human beings, he will transfer his trust to them and rely on them.

(*Tov Halevanon*: The author returned to the previous matter, and said that there are those who do not rely on their own resourcefulness, and they recognize their own lackings. However, they trust in the salvation from human beings. He thinks that he does not need to trust in anything more, and even if he becomes disabled and unable to provide for himself, they will not abandon him.)

(6) But when his wisdom grows and he realizes their lacking and their need for the Creator, he will then move his trust to G-d, and rely on Him for things beyond his own control and which he cannot escape submitting to the decree of G-d. For example, the falling of rainwater on the crops, or (safely) travelling through the sea, or crossing a barren desert, or floods, outbreaks of a plague among the living, or the like among matters which human beings have no plan whatsoever, as written: *"In the time of their trouble they will cry out: 'arise and save us' "* (Yirmiyahu 2:27).

(7) If his knowledge of G-d strengthens more, he will put his trust in G-d in matters where he has some plan, such as avoiding earning a livelihood through dangerous means or exhausting occupations that wear down the body, and trusts in G-d that He will provide for him through a lighter occupation.

(8) If his knowledge of G-d strengthens more, he will put his trust in G-d in all the means, whether difficult or easy, and while occupied in them, his intent will be directed to serve G-d and guard His commandments.

> (*Tov Halevanon*: i.e. He will put to heart, that G-d has no limitations, and He can provide the livelihood of every person through any means. And that which he is occupied with a specific trade, this is in order to observe the service of G-d, which He commanded us to engage in matters that cause our livelihood to come, and as the author wrote earlier [in chapter 4])

(9) If his knowledge of G-d strengthens more regarding His mercy on the created beings, he will accept with heart and mind, outwardly and inwardly, the decrees of G-d. He will rejoice in whatever G-d does to him, be it death or life, poverty or wealth, health or sickness. He will not desire other than what G-d has chosen for him, and desire only what G-d has chosen for him.

> (*Tov Halevanon*: i.e. he will acknowledge and bless G-d on the death of one of his relatives or children just like [he did] on their life, and likewise for poverty just like for wealth.

He will give himself over to G-d, and surrender his body and soul over to His judgment. He will not prefer one matter over another and will not choose anything other than his current situation, as one who trusts in G-d said: "I never resolved to do a thing and desired something else".

> (*Pas Lechem*: *"He will give himself over to G-d"* - regarding G-d's guidance of all of his needs.
> *"surrender his body and soul over to His judgment"* - If some bad thing happens to him, he receives it and bears it with a good countenance.
>
> *Manoach Halevavos*: He does not trust in one matter more than another. He does not think one matter is more profitable than another. All the causes and means are equal to him, because he realizes that they all depend on the will of G-d.

Therefore, he trusts only in G-d. Because of this, when he resolves to do something, he does not desire something else.

Matanas Chelko: this is the level of a true "baal bitachon" (truster in G-d). He does not trust in any means (even though he engages in them). Rather, he knows and believes that everything comes only from G-d. This level brings one to accept everything G-d decrees on him in all matters of life.)

(10) When his knowledge of G-d strengthens more than this and he understands the true intent why he was created and brought to this fleeting world, and he recognizes the exaltedness of the eternal, next world, he will think lightly of this world, and its means. With mind, soul, and body, he will flee from this world and surrender himself to the blessed Al-mighty, and delight in remembering Him in solitude. He will feel desolate when he is not (capable of - *MC*) meditating on His greatness.

(*Matanas Chelko*: this is an additional level of intensity of recognition and trust. Not only does he trust in G-d's ability and providence, but this recognition has brought him to strengthen his trust in the will of G-d. Now, he recognizes full well why he came to this world - not in order to work and make money, but only in order to do the will of G-d.

Manoach Halevavos: No thoughts come to his mind, except on the greatness of G-d. He is desolate and silent from other thoughts, and parts from them quickly if they enter his thoughts... He is astonished on those who do not contemplate. He thinks of the greatness of G-d always, and likewise he is amazed at himself if sometimes he does not meditate on the greatness of G-d, and he puts to heart that it is proper to think always of the greatness of G-d when sitting in his house, walking on the way, lying down, and rising up (a reference to the Shema).

Pas Lechem: When he is in solitude, away from people, and nothing distracts his thoughts, he will greatly delight in this because then he can remember Him with a focused mind.)

If he is among a crowd of people, he will long for nothing else than to do His will, and yearn only to come near to Him. His joy in his love of G-d will distract him from the pleasures worldly people have for this world, and even from the joy of souls in the next world.

> (*Tov Halevanon*: His joy in love of G-d will distract him to such an extent that he will not be able to enter in his heart any joy of worldly people, namely, the worldly matters they rejoice in.

> *Marpe Lenefesh*: His joy in love of G-d is greater than the pleasure of the living in reaching their desires and even greater than the pleasures of the dead in the next world, as our sages said (Avot 4:17): "one hour of repentance and good deeds in this world is better than all of the life of the next world")

This is the highest of the levels of those who trust in G-d, reached by the prophets, pious ones, and treasured, pure men of G-d, and this is what the verse refers to in saying: *"Even [for] the way of Your judgments, O L-ord, have we hoped for You; for Your Name and for Your remembrance is the desire of [our] soul directed"* (Isaiah 26:8), and *"my soul thirsts to the Al-mighty, the living G-d; [when shall I come and appear before G-d?]"* (Tehilim 42:3).

These are the ten levels of trust which one cannot escape belonging to one of them. We find the matter of trust in scripture expressed in 10 synonyms corresponding to these 10 levels. They are:
Mivtach (trust), Mishan (support), Tikva (hope), Machse (protection), Tochelet (waiting), Chikui (expecting), Semicha (reliance), Sever (resting), Misad (confidence), and Chesel (assurance).

May G-d place us among those who trust in Him, who give themselves over to His judgment outwardly and inwardly, in His mercy, Amen.

The Gate of trust is Complete, to G-d the Last and the First.

(*Translator*: some apt words from the introduction to the book "Path of the Just": "Therefore, the benefit to be gleaned from this book is not from a single reading... Rather the benefit derived [from this book] comes from review and diligent study..."

Rabbi Avigdor Miller zt'l: When the Chovos Halevavos speaks about bitachon, trusting in Hakodosh Boruch Hu, as the most essential of all requirements of avodas Hash-em, he's talking there about a very high level of bitachon; he means complete confidence in Hakodosh Boruch Hu - trusting in Him constantly, continuously and implicitly. In order to be a noble servant of Hash-em, then this confidence, this bitachon in Hakodosh Boruch Hu, is the most necessary requirement. Of course, the bitachon in the sense that the Chovos Halevavos is describing there is a sublime achievement that's very difficult to attain. Anybody who thinks that this bitachon that the Chovos Halevavos demands from us is a pashuteh (simple) subject, that it can be transmitted in a few words, then he never really studied it. *It needs a lot of work - you're going to have to meditate on the ways of Hakodosh Boruch Hu for a long time until you become saturated with the consciousness of Hakodosh Boruch Hu; with the paramount awareness that everything is under His control and that everything that He does is for good.* (from Toras Avigdor, Parsha Bamidbar, Order and Tranquility).

OTHER WORKS BY YOSEF SEBAG

Ethics of the Fathers   - www.dafyomireview.com/489

Duties of the Heart   - www.dafyomireview.com/384

Path of the Just   - www.dafyomireview.com/447

Gates of Holiness   - www.dafyomireview.com/442

Vilna Gaon on Yonah   - www.dafyomireview.com/259

Torah Numerology   - www.dafyomireview.com/543

Marks of Divine Wisdom - www.dafyomireview.com/427

Torah Authenticity   - www.dafyomireview.com/430

yosefsebag@gmail.com

Made in the USA
Monee, IL
23 September 2024

66390112R00105

חובות הלבבות
שער הבטחון

חובות הלבבות - שער הבטחון

~~ הקדמה ~~
בבטחון על האלהים יתברך לבדו.

אמר המחבר מפני שקדם מאמרנו בחיוב קבלת עבודת האלהים ראיתי
להביא אחריו מה שהוא צריך יותר מכל הדברים לעובד האלהים יתברך
והוא הבטחון עליו בכל דבריו בעבור מה שיש בו מן התועליות הגדולות
בענין התורה ובענין העולם.

ותועלותיו בו בתורתו

מהן מנוחת נפשו ובטחונו על אלהיו יתברך כמו שהעבד חיב לבטח על
אדוניו מפני שאם איננו בוטח באלהים בוטח בזולתו ומי שבוטח בזולת
יי מסיר האלהים השגחתו מעליו ומניח אותו ביד מי שבטח עליו ויהיה
כמו שנאמר בו (ירמיה ב יג) כי שתים רעות עשה עמי אותי עזבו מקור
מים חיים לחצב להם בארות בארות נשברים וגו', ואמר (תהלים קו כ)
וימירו את כבודם בתבנית שור אוכל עשב, ואמר הכתוב (ירמיה יז ז) ברוך
הגבר אשר יבטח בה' והיה ה' מבטחו, ואמר (תהלים מ ה) אשרי הגבר
אשר שם ה' מבטחו ולא פנה אל רהבים ושטי כזב, ואמר (ירמיה יז ה)
ארור הגבר אשר יבטח באדם ושם בשר זרועו ומן ה' יסור לבו.

ואם יבטח על חכמתו ותחבולותיו וכח גופו והשתדלותו ייגע לריק ויחלש
כחו ותקצר תחבולתו מהשיג חפצו כמו שאמר הכתוב (איוב ה יג) לוכד
חכמים בערמם, ואמר (קהלת ט יא) שבתי וראה תחת השמש, כי לא
לקלים המרוץ ולא לגבורים המלחמה וגו', ואמר (תהלים לד יא) כפירים
רשו ורעבו ודורשי ה' וגו'.

ואם יבטח ברוב עשרו יוסר ממנו וישאר לזולתו כמו שאמר הכתוב (איוב
כז יט) עשיר ישכב ולא יאסף עיניו פקח ואיננו, ואמר (משלי כג ד) אל תיגע
להעשיר מבינתך חדל, ואמר (משלי כג ה) התעיף עינך בו ואיננו וגו',
ואמר (ירמיה יז יא) בחצי ימיו יעזבנו וגו'.

או תמנע ממנו הנאתו בו כאשר אמר החכם (קהלת ו ב) ולא ישליטנו
האלהים וגו', ויהיה אצלו פקדון שישומר אותו מן הפגעים עד שישוב למי
שהוא ראוי לו כמו שאמר (קהלת ב כו) ולחוטא נתן ענין לאסף ולכנס לתת
לטוב לפני האלהים, ואמר (איוב כז יז) יכין וצדיק ילבש וכסף נקי יחלק.
ואפשר שיהיה הממון סבת רעתו ואבדן נפשו כמו שאמר הכתוב (קהלת

1

ה יב) יש רעה חולה ראיתי תחת השמש עשר שמור לבעליו לרעתו.

ומהם שהבוטח באלהים יביאנו הבטחתו עליו

שלא יעבד זולתו

ושלא יקוה לאיש ולא ייחל לבני אדם

ולא יעבדם להתרצות אליהם

ולא יחניף להם

ולא יסכים עמהם בבלתי עבודת האלהים

ולא יפחידהו ענינם

ולא יירא ממחלקותם

אבל יתפשט מבגדי טובותם וטרח הודאתם וחובת תגמולם

ואם יוכיח אותם לא יזהר בכבודם

ואם יכלימם לא יבוש מהם

ולא ייפה להם השקר

כמו שאמר הנביא (ישעיה נ ז) וה' אלהים יעזר לי על כן לא נכלמתי על כן שמתי פני כחלמיש ואדע כי לא אבוש, ואמר (יחזקאל ב ו) אל תירא מהם ומדבריהם אל תירא, ואמר (יחזקאל ב ו) מדבריהם אל תירא ומפניהם אל תחת, ואמר (ירמיה א ח) אל תירא מפניהם, ואמר (ירמיה א יז) אל תחת מפניהם, ואמר (יחזקאל ג ט) כשמיר חזק מצור נתתי מצחך וגו'.

ומהן שהבוטח באלהים יביאהו בטחונו לפנות את לבו מעניני העולם וליחד לבבו לעניני העבודה

ויהיה דומה במנוחת נפשו ורחב לבו ומעוט דאגתו לעניני עולמו לבעל האלכימיה והוא היודע להפך הכסף לזהב והנחשת והבדיל לכסף על ידי חכמה ומעשה.

2

ועוד כי הבוטח באלהים יש לו עליו יתרון בעשרה דברים:

תחלתם שבעל הכימיה צריך לדברים מיחדים למלאכה לא יגמר לו דבר
זולתם ולא ימצאם בכל עת ובכל מקום. והבוטח באלהים טרפו מבטח לו
מכל סבה מסבות העולם כמו שאמר הכתוב (דברים ח ג) למען הודיעך כי
לא על הלחם לבדו יחיה האדם וגו', כי הסבות אינן נבצרות ממנו בכל
עת ובכל מקום כאשר ידעת מדבר אליהו עם העורבים ועם האשה
האלמנה ועגת רצפים וצפחת המים ודבר עובדיהו עם הנביאים שאמר
(מלכים א' יח יג) ואחביא מנביאי ה' מאה איש חמשים חמשים איש
במערה ואכלכלם לחם ומים, ואמר (תהלים לד יא) כפירים רשו ורעבו
ודורשי ה' לא יחסרו כל טוב, ואמר (תהלים לד י) יראו את ה' קדושיו כי
אין מחסור ליראיו.

והשני כי בעל הכימיה צריך למעשים ולמלאכות לא ישלם לו חפצו
זולתם ואפשר שימיתוהו ריחם ועשנם עם התמדת העבודה ואורך
היגיעה בהם לילה ויומם. והבוטח באל בבטחה מהפגעים ולבו בטוח
ממצא הרעות וכל אשר יבואנו מאת האלהים יהיה לו לששון ולשמחה
וטרפו בא אליו במנוחה והשקט ושלוה כמו שכתוב (תהלים כג ב) בנאות
דשא ירביצני על מי מנוחות ינהלני.

והשלישי כי בעל הכימיה אינו מאמין על סודו זולתו מיראתו על נפשו.
והבוטח באלהים איננו ירא משום אדם בבטחונו אבל הוא מתפאר בו
כמו שאמר דוד המלך עליו השלום (תהלים נו יב) באלהים בטחתי לא
אירא מה יעשה אדם לי.

והרביעי כי בעל הכימיה אינו נמלט מהזמין מהזהב והכסף הרבה לעת
צרכו או שלא יזמין מהם כלום אלא כפי שיספיק לזמן מועט. ואם יזמין
ממנו הרבה יהיה כל ימיו מפחד על נפשו שלא יאבד ממנו במיני סבות
האבדה ולא ישקט לבו ולא תנוח נפשו מפחדו עליו מהמלך והעם. ואם
לא יזמין מהם אלא למלאת מחסורו זמן מעט אפשר שיבצר ממנו
המעשה בעת הצורך הגדול אליו מפני המנע סבה מסבותיו ממנו.
והבוטח באלהים בטחונו חזק באלהים שיטריף אותו כרצונו בעת שירצה
ובמקום שירצה כאשר יטריף העבר ברחם אמו והאפרוח בתוך הביצה
אשר אין בה מקום מפלש להכנס אליו ממנו דבר מחוצה והעוף באויר
והדגים במים והנמלה הקטנה עם חלישותה ויבצר הטרף מהארי עם
תקפו בקצת הימים כמו שכתוב (תהלים לד יא) כפירים רשו ורעבו וגו',
ואמר (משלי י ג) לא ירעיב ה' נפש צדיק וגו', ואמר (תהלים לז כה) נער

הייתי גם זקנתי ולא ראיתי צדיק נעזב וזרעו מבקש לחם.

והחמישי שבעל הכימיה תחת יראה ופחד על מלאכתו מן הגדול ועד הקטן שבעם. והבוטח באלהים ייראוהו הגדולים ונכבדי בני אדם אף החיות והאבנים מבקשים רצונו כמו שנאמר במזמור (תהלים צא א) יושב בסתר עליון עד אחריתו ואומר (איוב ה יט-כ) בשש צרות יצילך ובשבע לא יגע בך רע ברעב פדך ממות עד סוף הענין.

והששי שבעל הכימיה אינו בטוח מהחליים והמדוים שמערבבין עליו שמחתו בעשרו ואינם מניחין אותו להנות ממה שיש לו ולא להתענג במה שהשיגה ידו. והבוטח ביי בטוח מן המדוים והחליים אלא על דרך הכפרה או על דרך התמורה כמו שכתוב (ישעיה מ ל) ויעפו נערים ויגעו ובחורים כשל יכשלו, ואמר (ישעיה מ לא) וקוי ה' יחליפו כח וגו', ואמר (תהלים לז יז) כי זרועות רשעים תשברנה וגו'.

והשביעי שבעל הכימיה אפשר שלא יגיע אל מזונו במה שיש אצלו מן הזהב והכסף מפני שלא יהיה האכל נמצא בעירו בקצת העתים כמה שנאמר (יחזקאל ז יט) כספם בחוצות ישליכו, ואמר (צפניה א יח) גם כספם גם זהבם לא יוכל להצילם. והבוטח ביי לא יבצר ממנו מזונו בכל עת ובכל מקום עד סוף ימיו כמו שנאמר (איוב ה כ) ברעב פדך ממות וגו', ואמר (תהלים כג א) ה' רועי לא אחסר וגו', ואמר (תהלים לז יט) לא יבשו בעת רעה ובימי רעבון ישבעו.

והשמיני שבעל הכימיה איננו מתעכב בשום מקום מיראתו שמא יתגלה סודו. והבוטח באלהים בבטחה בארצו ובמנוחת נפש במקומו כמו שכתוב (תהלים לז ג) בטח בה' ועשה טוב שכן ארץ ורעה אמונה, ואמר (תהלים לז כט) צדיקים יירשו ארץ וישכנו לעד עליה.

והתשיעי שבעל הכימיה לא תלונו הכימיה שלו באחריתו ולא ישיג בה בעולם הזה זולת הבטחון מן הריש והצרך לבני אדם. והבוטח ביי ילונו גמול בטחונו בעולם הזה ולעולם הבא כמו שכתוב (תהלים לב י) והבוטח בה' חסד יסובבנו, ואמר (תהלים לא כ) מה רב טובך אשר צפנת ליראיך וגו'.

והעשירי שבעל הכימיה אם יודע ענינו תהיה סבת מותו מפני שמה שהוא משתדל וטורח בו הפך הנהגת העולם ומנהיג הכל ישליט עליו מי שימיתהו כשאינו יודע להעלים את סודו. והבוטח ביי כאשר יודע בטחונו יגדל בעיני הבריות ויכבדוהו בני אדם ויתברכו בקרבתו ובראייתו ויהיה

גורם לתקנת עירו ולדחות הפגעים מעל אנשי מקומו כמו שכתוב (משלי י
כה) וצדיק יסוד עולם, וכענין לוט בצוער.

ומתועלת הבטחון בה' בענין התורה

כי הבוטח ביי אם הוא בעל ממון ימהר להוציא חובות האלהים וחובות
בני אדם מממונו בנפש חפצה ורוח נדיבה. ואם איננו בעל ממון יראה כי
חסרון הממון טובה מטובות המקום עליו מפני שנסתלקו מעליו החובות
שהוא חיב בהם לאלהים ולבני אדם בעבורו ומעוט טרדת לבו בשמירתו
והנהגתו כמו שנאמר על אחד מן החסידים שהיה אומר המקום יצילני
מפזור הנפש. אמרו לו מה הוא פזור הנפש? אמר שיהיה לי ממון בראש
כל נהר ובראש כל קריה, והוא מה שאמרו ז"ל (משנה אבות ב ז) מרבה
נכסים מרבה דאגה, ואמרו (משנה אבות ד א) איזהו עשיר השמח בחלקו.

והבוטח ביי ישיג תועלת הממון רצוני לומר פרנסתו ותמנע ממנו טרדת
המחשבה של בעל הממון והתמדת דאגתו לו כמו שאמר החכם (קהלת ה
יא) .

ומהן כי הבוטח ביי לא ימנענו רב הממון מבטח ביי מפני שאיננו סומך
על הממון והוא בעיניו כפקדון צוה להשתמש בו על פנים מיחדים
ובענינים מיחדים לזמן קצוב. ואם יתמיד קיומו אצלו לא יבעט בעבורו
ולא יזכיר טובתו למי שצוה לתת לו ממנו ולא יבקש עליו גמול הודאה
ושבח אבל הוא מודה לבוראו יתברך אשר שמהו סבה לטובות.

ואם יאבד הממון ממנו לא ידאג ולא יאבל לחסרונו אך הוא מודה לאלהיו
בקחתו פקדונו מאתו כאשר הודה בנתינתו לו וישמח בחלקו ואיננו
מבקש הזק זולתו ולא יחמד אדם בממונו כמו שאמר החכם (משלי יג כה)
צדיק אוכל לשובע נפשו.

אך תועלות הבטחון בעולם

מהן מנוחת הלב מן הדאגות העולמיות

והשלוה מנדנוד הנפש וצערה לחסרון תאוותיה הגופיות

והוא בהשקט ובבטחה ובשלוה בעולם הזה כמו שכתוב (ירמיה יז ז) ברוך
הגבר אשר יבטח בה' והיה ה' מבטחו, ואמר (ירמיה יז ח) והיה כעץ
שתול על מים ועל יובל ישלח שרשיו וגו'.

5

ומהן מנוחת הנפש מלכת בדרכים הרחוקים אשר היא מכלה הגופות וממהרת השלמת ימי החיים כמו שנאמר (תהלים קב כד) ענה בדרך כחי קצר ימי.

ונאמר על אחד מן הפרושים כי הלך אל ארץ רחוקה לבקש הטרף בתחלת פרישותו ופגע אדם אחד מעובדי כוכבים בעיר אשר הלך אליה. אמר לו הפרוש כמה אתם בתכלית העורון ומעוט ההבנה בעבודתכם לכוכבים. אמר לו האמגושי ומה אתה עובד? אמר לו הפרוש אני עובד הבורא היכול, המכלכל האחד, המטריף, אשר אין כמוהו. אמר לו האמגושי פעלך סותר את דבריך. אמר לו הפרוש והיאך? אמר לו אילו היה מה שאמרת אמת, היה מטריפך בעירך, כמו שהטריפך הנה, ולא היית טורח לבוא אל ארץ רחוקה כזאת. ונפסקה טענת הפרוש ושב לארצו וקבל הפרישות מן העת ההיא ולא יצא מעירו אחר כך.

ומהן מנוחת הנפש והגוף מן המעשים הקשים והמלאכות המיגעות את הגופות ועזב עבודת המלכים וחקיהם וחמס אנשיהם.

והבוטח ביי הוא תובע מסבות הטרף מה שיש בו יותר מנוחה לגופו ושם טוב לו ופנאי ללבו ומה שהוא מפיק יותר לחובות תורתו עם יתר אמונתו כי הסבה לא תוסיף לו בחקו ולא תחסרהו ממנו מאומה אלא בגזרת האלהים יתברך כמו שנאמר (תהלים עה ז-ח) לא ממוצא וממערב ולא ממדבר הרים כי אלהים שופט זה ישפיל וזה ירים, ואמר (תהלים כג ב) בנאות דשא ירביצני על מי מנוחות ינהלני.

ומהן מעוט צער נפשו במסחרו ואם תתעכב אצלו פרקמטיא או אם לא יוכל לגבות חובו או אם יפגעהו חלי בגופו מפני שהוא יודע כי הבורא יתברך מתקן ענינו יותר ממנו ובוחר לו טוב יותר ממה שהוא בוחר לעצמו כמו שנאמר (תהלים סב ו) אך לאלהים דומי נפשי כי ממנו תקותי.

ומהן שמחתו בכל ענין שיעתק אליו ואם יהיה כנגד טבעו מפני בטחונו באלהים שלא יעשה לו אלא הטוב לו בכל ענין כאשר תעשה האם החומלת לבנה ברחיצתו וחתולו וקשרתו והתרתו על כרחו כמו שאמר דוד עליו השלום (תהלים קלא ב) אם לא שויתי ודוממתי נפשי כגמול עלי אמו כגמול עלי נפשי.

וכיון שבארתי מתועלות הבטחון באלהים והנאותיו בתורה ובעולם מה שנזדמן לי אבאר עתה מענין הבטחון שבעה דברים:

אחד מהם מה הוא הבטחון. והשני בסבות סבות הבטחון על הברואים. והשלישי בבאור ההקדמות אשר בעבורן יתחייב הבטחון באלהים וחיוב העסק בסבות. והרביעי בבאור הדברים אשר בהם יהיה הבטחון וחיוב שבחו וגנותו בהם. והחמישי בהפרש שיש בין עסק הבוטח באלהים בסבות הטרף ובין עסק מי שאינו בוטח באלהים בהם. והששי בבאור אפני חיוב גנות דעת האומרים באריכות התאוות בעולם ומיחלים נפשותם בקבלת עבודת האלהים כשיגיעו לחפצם בו והם בעלי המשכונות. והשביעי במפסידי הבטחון באלהים וכל מה שצריך לדבר בענין הבטחון ולקצר בחלקיו.

~~ פרק א ~~

אך מהות הבטחון היא מנוחת נפש הבוטח ושיהיה לבו סמוך על מי שבטח עליו שיעשה הטוב והנכון לו בענין אשר יבטח עליו כפי יכלתו ודעתו ובמה שמפיק טובתו.

אבל העקר אשר בעבורו יהיה הבטחון מן הבוטח ואם יפקד לא ימצא הבטחון הוא שיהיה לבו בטוח במי שיבטח בו שיקים מה שאמר ויעשה מה שערב ויחשב עליו הטוב במה שלא התנה לו ולא ערב בעשותו שיעשהו ונדבה הוא וחסד.

~~ פרק ב ~~

אך הסבות אשר בהן יתכן הבטחון מהבוטח על הברואים הן שבע.

אחת מהן הרחמים והחמלה והאהבה. כי האדם כשהוא יודע אויודע בחברו שהוא מרחם וחומל עליו יבטח בו ותנוח נפשו עליו לכל מה שיטריחהו בעניניו.

והשנית שיהיה יודע בו עם אהבתו שאיננו מתעלם ממנו ולא מתעצל בחפצו אבל הוא יודע בו שהוא משתדל ומסכים לעשותו. כי אם לא יתברר לו ממנו כל זה לא יהיה בטחונו עליו שלם מפני שהוא יודע התעלמותו ורפיונו בחפצו.

וכאשר יתקבצו לבוטח ממי שבטח בו אלה מדות יתי שתי אלה גדל רחמנותו עליו ורב השגחתו על עניניו יבטח בו מבלי ספק.

והשלישית שיהיה שיהיה חזק לא ינצח באשר הוא חפץ ולא ימנעהו מונע מעשותו בקשת הבוטח. כי אם יהיה חלש לא ישלם הבטחון עליו אף על

7

פי שנתברר שהוא מרחם ומשגיח מפני המנע דברים ממנו ברב
העניניים. וכאשר יתקבצו בו שלש המדות האלה יהיה הבטחון עליו יותר
ראוי.

והרביעית שיהיה יודע באפני תועלת הבוטח עליו ולא יעלם ממנו מה
שהוא טוב לו בנסתר ובנראה ומה שייטב בו ענינו. כי אם לא ידע כל זה
לא תנוח נפש הבוטח עליו. וכאשר יתקבצו לו בו דעתו בתועלותיו ויכלתו
בהם ורב השגחתו עליהן וחמלתו עליו יחזק בטחונו בו מבלי ספק.

והחמישית שיהיה מתיחד בהנהגת הבוטח עליו מתחלת הויתו וגדולו
וינקותו ונערותו ובחרותו וישישותו וזקנתו עד תכלית ענינו. וכשיתברר
כל זה ממנו לבוטח יתחיב שתנוח נפשו עליו וישען עליו בעבור מה
שקדם לו עליו מן הטובות העודפות והתועליות המתמידות ויהיה זה
מחיב חזקת בטחונו בו.

והששית שיהיה ענין הבוטח כלו מסור בידו ולא יוכל אדם להזיקו
ולהועילו ולא להטיב אליו ולא לדחות נזק מעליו זולתו כעבד האסור
אשר הוא בבית הבור ברשות אדוניו. וכשיהיה הבוטח ברשות מי שבטח
עליו על הענין הזה יהיה יותר ראוי לבטח עליו.

והשביעית שיהיה מי שבטח עליו בתכלית הנדיבות והחסד למי שראוי
לו ולמי שאינו ראוי לו ותהיה נדיבותו מתמדת וחסדו נמשך לא יכרת ולא
יפסק.

ומי שנקבצו בו כל המדות האלה עם כל מה שהזכרנו קודם לזה נשלמו
תנאי הבטחון בו והתחיב בו היודע זה ממנו לבטח בו ושתנוח נפשו עליו
בגליו ובנסתרו בלבו ובאבריו ולהמסר אליו ולרצות בגזרותיו ולדון אותו
לטוב בכל דיניו ומפעליו.

וכאשר נחקר על אלה השבעה תנאים לא נמצאם כלל בברואים ונמצאם
כלם בבורא יתעלה. שהוא מרחם על בריותיו כמו שכתוב (תהלים קג ח)
רחום וחנון ה' וגו', ואמר (יונה ד יא) ואני לא אחוס על נינוה העיר הגדולה
וגו'.

ושאינו מתעלם כמו שכתוב (תהלים קכא ד) הנה לא ינום ולא יישן שומר
ישראל. ושהוא חכם ולא ינצח כמו שכתוב (איוב ט ד) חכם לבב ואמיץ כח
מי הקשה אליו וישלם, ואמר (דברי הימים א כט יא) לך ה' הגדולה והגבורה
והתפארת והנצח וההוד וגו', וכתיב (צפניה ג יז) ה' אלהיך בקרבך גבור

8

יושיע.

ושהוא מתיחד בהנהגת האדם מתחלת ענינו והתחלת גדולו כמו
שנאמר (דברים לב ו) הלא הוא אביך קנך הוא עשך ויכננך, ואמר (תהלים
עא ו) עליך נסמכתי מבטן ממעי אמי אתה גוזי, ואמר (איוב י י) הלא כחלב
תתיכני וכגבינה תקפיאני, ושאר הענין.

ושתועלתו והזקו אינם ברשות אדם כי אם ביד הבורא יתעלה לבדו כמו
שנאמר (איכה ג לז-לח) מי זה אמר ותהי ה' לא צוה מפי עליון לא תצא
הרעות והטוב, ואמר (ישעיה מ ח) יבש חציר נבל ציץ ודבר אלהינו יקום
לעולם, ואמר (ישעיה מ ז) אכן חציר העם. וכבר התברר הענין הזה
במאמר השלישי מן הספר הזה במה שיש בו די

ושנדיבותו כוללת וחסדו סובב כמו שנאמר (תהלים קמה ט) טוב ה' לכל
ורחמיו על כל מעשיו, ואמר (תהלים קלו כה) נותן לחם לכל בשר כי לעולם
חסדו, ואמר (תהלים קמה טז) פותח את ידך ומשביע לכל חי רצון.

והשכל גוזר בהקבץ אלה השבעה ענינים בבורא יתעלה מבלתי
הנבראים לכן הבאתי אלו הפסוקים מן הכתוב לזכרון בלבד.

וכאשר יתברר זה לאדם ותתחזק הכרתו באמתת חסד הבורא יבטח בו
וימסר אליו ויניח הנהגתו עליו ולא יחשדהו בדינו ולא יתקצף על בחירתו
לו כמו שאמר דוד עליו השלום (תהלים קטז יג) כוס ישועות אשא ובשם ה'
אקרא, ואמר (תהלים קטז ג-ד) צרה ויגון אמצא ובשם ה' אקרא.

~~ פרק ג ~~
אך ההקדמות אשר בברורן ואמתתן ישלם לאדם הבטחון באלהים הן
חמש.

אחת מהן שיאמין ויתברר אצלו התקבצות השבעה ענינים באלהים אשר
בהתקבצם במי שבוטחים בו יתכן לבטח עליו. וכבר זכרתים והעירותי
עליהם במה שנזדמן לי מן הכתוב והם

הראשון שהבורא יתברך מרחם על האדם יותר מכל מרחם וכל רחמים
וחמלה שיהיו מזולתו עליו כלם הם מרחמי האל וחמלתו כמו שאמר
הכתוב (דברים יג יח) ונתן לך רחמים ורחמך והרבך.

והשני כי הבורא יתעלה לא יעלמו ממנו אפני תועלת האדם והדין נותן

9

זה מפני שהוא אחד ממעשיו ואין מי שיודע באפני תקנות העשוי והפסדו ובפגעים המשיגים אותו ובאפני מחלתו וארוכתו יותר מעושהו.

ואם יהיה זה נמצא בעושים מבני אדם אשר לא יחדשו במעשיהם זולתי צורה מקרית אך השרש והצורה העצמית אין להם בהם שום תחבולה ולא יכלת לחדשם

ואשר חדש שרש האדם וצורתו ותכונתו וסדר חבורו הוא החכם היודע בעניני תעלותיו ונזקיו והטוב לו בעולמו ואחריתו בלי ספק כמו שכתוב (ישעיה מח יז) אני ה' אלהיך מלמדך להועיל מדריכך בדרך תלך, ואמר (משלי ג יב) כי את אשר יאהב ה' יוכיח וגו'.

והשלישי כי הבורא יתברך חזק מכל חזק ודברו נגזר מכל דבר ואין משיב דינו כמו שנאמר (תהלים קלה ו) כל אשר חפץ ה' עשה, ואמר (ישעיה נה יא) כן יהיה דברי אשר יצא מפי לא ישוב אלי ריקם וגו'.

והרביעי כי הוא משגיח על הנהגת עניני האדם כלם לא יניחם ולא יתעלם מהם ולא יסתר ממנו דבר מהם מקטנם ועד גדולם ולא ישכיחהו דבר את דבר כמו שכתוב (ישעיה מ כז) למה תאמר יעקב ותדבר ישראל נסתרה דרכי מה' ומאלהי משפטי יעבר, ואמר (ישעיה מ כח) הלוא ידעת אם לא שמעת אלהי עולם ה' בורא קצות הארץ לא ייעף ולא ייגע אין חקר לתבונתו.

והחמישי שאין ביד אחד מהברואים להועיל את נפשו ולא להזיקה ולא לזולתו כי אם ברשות הבורא יתברך.

כי העבד כשיהיה לו יותר מאדון אחד ויהיה כל אחד מהם יכול להועילו לא יתכן לו לבטח על אחד מהם מפני שמקוה התועלת מכל אחד מהם. ואם יהיה אחד מהם יכול על תועלתו יותר משאריתם יהיה חזק בטחונו בו כפי יכלתו אף על פי שהוא בוטח בשאריתם. ואם לא יוכל להועילו ולהזיקו כי אם אחד מהם בלבד על כרחו יבטח עליו לבדו מפני שאינו מקוה תועלת מזולתו. וכן כשירגיש האדם שלא יועילנו ולא יזיקנו אחד מהנבראים אלא ברשות הבורא יתברך ישוב לבו מיראתם ותקותם ויבטח על הבורא לבדו כמו שנאמר (תהלים קמו ג) אל תבטחו בנדיבים בבן אדם שאין לו תשועה.

והששי שידע רב טוב האלהים על האדם ומה שהתחיל אותו בו מרב החסד והטובה מבלי שיהיה ראוי אצלו לכך ולא לצרך שיהיה אליו אך

נדבה וטובה וחסד כאשר בארנו בשער הבחינה מן הספר הזה וכמו שאמר דוד עליו השלום (תהלים מ ו) רבות עשית אתה ה' אלהי נפלאותיך ומחשבותיך אלינו אין ערוך אליך אגידה ואדברה עצמו מספר.

והשביעי שיתברר אצלו כי יש לכל ההויות שבעולם הזה מעצם ומקרה גבול ידוע ולא יוסיף ולא יגרע על מה שגזר הבורא יתברך בכמותו ואיכותו וזמנו ומקומו אין מרבה למה שגזר במעוטו ולא ממעט ממה שגזר ברבותו ולא מאחר למה שגזר להקדימו ולא מקדים למה שגזר לאחרו. ומה שיהיה מן הדברים על ההפך מזה הוא הנגזר אשר קדם בתחלת הידיעה אלא שלכל הגזרות הקודמות בידיעת הבורא סבות ולסבות סבות.

ומי שאינו מבין מביני עניני העולם יחשב כי הסבה המתחדשת מחיבת שנוי הענינים והתהפכותם מענין אל ענין. והסבה חלושה ונקלה מהיות ממנה שנוי או חלוף בעצמם כאשר נראה הגרגיר האחד מן החטה מצמיח שלש מאות שבלים ובכל שבלת שלשים גרגרים ויהיה הגרגיר האחד סבה לעשרת אלפים או קרוב להם. היעלם כי כח הגרגיר חלוש מעשות כמות זו וכן שאר הגרגרים הנזרעים והנטועים. וכן נאמר בהיות האדם ושאר החיים מטפת הזרע וכמו כן הוית הדג הגדול מביצת הדג עם קטנותה.

וטרדת הנפש להקדים מה שאחר הבורא יתעלה ולאחר מה שהקדים ולהרבות מה שהמעיט ולהמעיט מה שהרבה מקניני העולם מבלי סבב אל קיום מצות עבודתו וקבול תורתו חלישות ההכרה באמתת ידיעתו וסכלות מהבין טובות הנהגתו.

וכבר רמז החכם אל הענין הזה במאמרו (קהלת ג א) לכל זמן ועת לכל חפץ תחת השמים, ואחר כך זכר מהם עשרים ושמונה ענינים והוא מה שאמר (קהלת ג ב) עת ללדת ועת למות וגו' עד אמרו (קהלת ג ח) עת מלחמה ועת שלום, ואמר (קהלת ט יא) כי עת ופגע יקרה את כלם, ואמר (קהלת ה ז) כי גבוה מעל גבוה שומר וגבוהים עליהם.

והליכות דיני הבורא יתעלה יותר נעלמות ועמקות ועליונות מהגיע אל ידיעת חלקיהן כל שכן כללן. וכבר אמר הכתוב (ישעיה נה ט) כי גבהו שמים מארץ כן גבהו דרכי מדרכיכם ומחשבותי ממחשבותיכם.

וההקדמה השנית שידע ויתברר אצלו כי הבורא יתברך משקיף עליו ואין נעלם ממנו נגלהו ונסתרו וצפונו ונראהו ואם בטחונו באלהיו בלב שלם

11

אם לא כאשר אמר הכתוב (תהלים צד יא) ה' יודע מחשבות אדם כי המה הבל, ואמר (משלי כד יב) הלא תוכן לבות הוא יבין, ואמר (מלכים א ח לט) כי אתה ידעת לבדך את לבב כל בני האדם.

וכשיתברר זה לבוטח אין ראוי לו לטעון שהוא בוטח באלהים יתעלה בדבורו מבלי שיבטח עליו בלבו ובמצפונו ויהיה במעלת מי שנאמר עליהם (ישעיה כט יג) בפיו ובשפתיו כבדוני ולבו רחק ממני.

וההקדמה השלישית שייחד אליהו בבטחונו בו במה שהוא חיב לבטח בו ואל ישתתף זולתו עמו ויבטח עליו ועל אחד מהברואים ויפסד בטחונו באלהיו בהשתתף זולתו עמו. וכבר ידעת מה שנאמר באסא עם חסידותו עת שסמך על הרופאים דכתיב (דברי הימים ב טז יב) ובחליו לא דרש את ה' כי אם ברופאים, ונענש על זה ואמר הכתוב (ירמיה יז ז) ברוך הגבר אשר יבטח בה' והיה ה' מבטחו.

ומן הידוע כי מי שימנה מבני אדם שני ממנים או יותר לעשות דבר מנויו מפסד כל שכן מי שבטח על האלהים וזולתו שיסתר בטחונו

ויהיה זה הסבה החזקה להמנע ממנו מה שבטח עליו כמו שאמר (ירמיה יז ה) ארור הגבר אשר יבטח באדם ושם בשר זרעו ומן ה' יסור לבו.

וההקדמה הרביעית שתהיה השגחתו והשתדלותו גדולה לקים מה שחיבו בו הבורא מעבודתו ולעשות מצוותיו ולהזהר מאשר הזהירו ממנו כפי מה שהוא מבקש שיהיה הבורא מסכים לו במה שהוא בוטח עליו בו כמו שאמרו רבותינו זכרונם לברכה (משנה אבות ב ד) עשה רצונו כרצונך כדי שיעשה רצונך כרצונו, בטל רצונך מפני רצונו כדי שיבטל רצון אחרים מפני רצונך.

ואמר הכתוב (תהלים לז ב) בטח בה' ועשה טוב שכן ארץ ורעה אמונה, ואמר (איכה ג כה) טוב ה' לקויו לנפש תדרשנו.

אבל מי שיבטח על הבורא והוא ממרה אותו כמה הוא סכל וכמה דעתו חלושה והכרתו כי הוא רואה כי מי שנתמנה לו מבני אדם על דבר כשהוא מצוה אותו להתעסק בצרך מצרכיו או מזהיר אותו מדבר ויעבר על מצותיו ויגיע לממנה עברו על מצותו כי יהיה הסבה החזקה להמנע ממנו העשות מה שבטח עליו בו. כל שכן מי שעבר על חקי האלהים ומצותיו אשר יעד והעיד עליהם שתהיה תוחלת הבוטח עליו נכזבה כשימרהו ולא יהיה ראוי להקרא בשם בוטח באלהים אך הוא כמו

שאמר הכתוב (איוב כז ח-ט) כי מה תקות חנף כי יבצע כי ישל אלוה נפשו הצעקתו ישמע אל, ואמר (ירמיה ז ט) הגנב רצח ונאף והשבע לשקר, ואמר (ירמיה ז י) ובאתם ועמדתם לפני בבית הזה אשר נקרא שמי עליו, ואמר (ירמיה ז יא) המערת פריצים היה הבית הזה אשר נקרא שמי עליו.

וההקדמה החמישית שיתבאר אצלו כי השלמת הדברים המתחדשים בעולם הזה לאחר היצירה הוא בשני דברים:

אחד מהם גזרות הבורא יתעלה וחפצו ביציאתם אל גבול ההויה

והשני סבות ומצועים מהם קרובים ומהם רחוקים ומהם נגלים ומהם נסתרים וכלם רצים להשלים מה שנגזר הויתו והראאותו בעזר האלהים להם על זה.

ודמיון הסבות הקרובות כהוצאת המים ממעמקי הארץ בגלגל בכלים המעלים את המים מן הבאר וסבתו הרחוקה האדם שהוא קושר הבהמה אל הגלגל ומניעתו להעלות המים מתחתיות הבאר אל פני הארץ.

אך הסבות אשר בין האדם והכלים מצועים בין שני הדברים והם הבהמה והעגולים שמניע קצתם את קצתם והחבל. ואם יקרה פגע לאחת מן הסבות הנזכרות לא יגמר הענין המכון בהם.

וכן שאר המעשים היוצאים אל גבול ההויה לא יתקבצו מן האדם וזולתו כי אם בגזרת האלהים והזמנתו הסבות אשר בהן הגמרם כמו שאמר (שמואל א ב ג) ולו נתכנו עלילות, ואמר (ירמיה לב יט) גדול העצה ורב העליליה, ואמר (מלכים א יב טו) כי היתה סבה מעם ה'. ואם תהיינה הסבות נעדרות בכלל לא תגמר יציאת דבר מן הפעלות הטבעיות אל גדר ההויה.

וכאשר נסתכל בצרך האדם לסבב ולהתגלגל לגמר ענינו נמצאהו בראות העין. כי הצריך אל המזון כשיושם לפניו המאכל כראוי לו אם לא יתגלגל לאכלו בהגבהתו אל פיו ולעסו לא ישבר רעבונו. וכן הצמא בצרכו אל המים וכל שכן אם ימנע המאכל ממנו עד שיתגלגל לתקנו בטחינה ולישה ואפיה והדומה לזה. ויותר גלגול מזה וקשה אם יצטרך לקנותה ולתקנו. ויותר מזה עוד אם לא יזדמנו לו הדמים שיקנה אותו בהם ויצטרך לגלגול ולסבוב גדול ממה שזכרנו קדם שישתכר בדמים או שימכר מה שהוא צריך לו מחפצים וקנינים וכיוצא בהם. והעלה אשר

13

בעבורה חיב הבורא את האדם לחזר ולסבב על סבות הטרף ושאר מה שהוא צריך אליו לשני פנים.

אחד מהם מפני שחיבה החכמה בחינת הנפש בעבודת האלהים ובהמרותו בחן אותה במה שמראה זה ממנה והוא הצרך והחסרון אל מה שהוא חוץ לה ממאכל ומשתה ומלבוש ומעון ומשגל וצוה אותם לחזר עליהם להביאם בסבות המוכנות להם על פנים מיחדים ועתים ידועים.

ומה שגזר הבורא שיגמר לאדם מהם יגמר וישלם בהשלמת הזדמנות הסבות.

ואשר לא גזר לו להגמר בהם לא יגמר וימנעו ממנו הסבות.

ונתבררו ממנו העבודה והעברה בכונה ובבחירה לאחת מהנה מבלתי האחרת ויתחיב אחר זה הגמול והענש ואפלו לא גמר בהם המעשה.

והשני כי אלו לא הצרך האדם לטרח ולחזר ולסבב להבאת טרפו היה בועט ורודף אחר העברות ולא היה משגיח על מה שהוא חיב בו על טובת האלהים עליו כמו שנאמר (ישעיה ה יב) והיה כנור ונבל תף וחליל יין משתיהם ואת פועל ה' לא יביטו ומעשה ידיו לא ראו, ואמר (דברים לב טו) וישמן ישורון ויבעט שמנת עבית כשית ויטש אלוה עשהו. ואמרו זכרונם לברכה (משנה אבות ב ב) יפה תלמוד תורה עם דרך ארץ שיגיעת שניהם משכחת עון וכל תורה שאין עמה מלאכה סופה בטלה וגוררת עון. וכל שכן מי שאין לו חלק באחת מהן ולא שם לבו על אחת מהן.

והיה מחמלת הבורא יתעלה על האדם שהטרידו בעניני עולמו ואחריתו להתעסק כל ימי חייו בזה ולא יבקש מה שאינו צריך לו ולא יוכל להשיגו בשכלו כמו עניני ההתחלה והתכלה כמו שאמר החכם (קהלת ג יא) גם את העולם נתן בלבם מבלי אשר לא ימצא האדם את המעשה אשר עשה האלהים מראש ועד סוף.

ואם הוא מגביר עבודת האלהים ובוחר ביראתו ובוטח בו בעניני תורתו ועולמו וסר מן הדברים המגנים וכוסף למדות הטובות לא יבעט במנוחה ולא יטה אל השלוה ולא ישיאהו היצר ולא יפת בכשפי העולם יסתלק מעליו טרח הגלגול והסבוב בהבאת טרפו מפני הסתלקות שני הפנים הנזכרים מעליו הבחינה והבעיטה בטובה ויבואהו טרפו בלי טרח ובלי יגיעה כפי ספוקו ומזונו כמו שנאמר (משלי י ג) לא ירעיב ה' נפש צדיק.

ואם יאמר האומר הנה אנחנו רואים מקצת צדיקים לא יזדמן להם טרפם אלא אחרי העמל והיגיעה ורבים מאנשי העברות בשלוה וחייהם בטוב ובנעימים.

נאמר כי כבר קדמו הנביאים והחסידים לחקר על זה הענין מהם מי שאמר (ירמיה יב א) מדוע דרך רשעים צלחה, ואמר האחר (חבקוק א ג) למה תראני און ועמל תביט ושוד וחמס לנגדי ויהי ריב ומדון ישא, ואמר (חבקוק א ד) כי רשע מכתיר את הצדיק, ואמר (חבקוק א יג) תחריש בבלע רשע צדיק ממנו, ואמר אחר (תהלים עג יב) הנה אלה רשעים ושלוי עולם השגו חיל, ואמר (תהלים עג יג-יד) אך ריק זכיתי לבבי וארחץ בנקיון כפי ואהי נגוע כל היום ותוכחתי לבקרים. ואמר אחר על אנשי דורו (מלאכי ג טו) גם בחנו אלהים וימלטו, והרבה כזה.

אך הניח הנביא התשובה בבאור עלת זה מפני שעלת כל אחד מן הצדיקים הנבחנים. וכל אחד מן הרשעים שהם בטובה בעולם הזה זולת עלת האחר לכן העיר על זה באמרו (דברים כט כח) הנסתרות לה׳ אלהינו והנגלות לנו ולבנינו, ואמר החכם בדומה לזה (קהלת ה ז) אם עשק רש וגזל משפט וצדק תראה במדינה אל תתמה וגו', ואמר הכתוב (דברים לב ד) הצור תמים פעלו כי כל דרכיו משפט.

ועם כל זה ראיתי לבאר בענין הזה מה שהיה בו מעט הספקה.

ואמר כי הפנים אשר בעבורם ימנע מהצדיק הזדמנות טרפו עד שיטרח עליו ויבחן בו

אפשר שיהיה עון שקדם לו התחיב להפרע ממנו עליו כמו שנאמר (משלי יא לא) הן צדיק בארץ ישולם.

ויש שיהיה על דרך התמורה בעולם הבא כמו שכתוב (דברים ח טז) להיטבך באחריתך.

ויש שיהיה להראות סבלו והסברתו הטובה בעבודת הבורא יתברך כדי שילמדו בני אדם ממנו כמו שידעת מענין איוב.

ויש שיהיה לרשעי אנשי דורו ויבחנהו הבורא יתעלה בעני ובריש ובחלאים להראות חסידותו ועבודתו לאלהים מבלעדיהם כמו שנאמר (ישעיה נג ד) אכן חלינו הוא נשא ומכאובינו סבלם.

15

ויש שיהיה מפני שאיננו מקנא לאלהים לקחת הדין מאנשי דורו כמו
שידעת מענין עלי ובניו שאמר בהם הכתוב (שמואל א ב לו) והיה כל
הנותר בביתך יבוא להשתחות לו וגו'.

אבל טובת האל יתברך על הרשע יש שתהיה בעבור טובה שקדמה לו
יגמלהו האלהים עליה בעולם הזה כמו שאמר (דברים ז י) ומשלם לשונאיו
אל פניו להאבידו, ותרגמו בו הראשונים ומשלם לשנאוהי זכוון דאינון
עבדין קדמוהי בחייהון לאובדיהון.

ויש שתהיה על דרך הפקדון אצלו עד שיתן לו האל יתברך בן צדיק יהיה
ראוי לה כמו שאמר (איוב כז יז) יכין וצדיק ילבש, ואמר (קהלת ב כו)
ולחוטא נתן ענין לאסף ולכנס לתת לטוב לפני האלהים.

ואפשר שתהיה הסבה הגדולה שבסבות מותו ורעתו כמו שכתוב (קהלת
ה יב) עושר שמור לבעליו לרעתו.

ואפשר שתהיה להאריך הבורא יתעלה לו עד שישוב ויהיה ראוי לה כמו
שידעת מענין מנשה.

ויש שתהיה לחסד שקדם אביו והיה ראוי להטיב לבנו בעבורו כמו
שאמר ליהוא בן נמשי (מלכים ב י ל) בני רבעים ישבו לך על כסא ישראל,
ואמר (משלי כ ז) מתהלך בתומו צדיק אשרי בניו אחריו, ואמר (תהלים לז
כה) נער הייתי גם זקנתי ולא ראיתי צדיק נעזב וזרעו מבקש לחם.

ויש שתהיה לנסות אנשי התרמית והמצפונים הרעים כשהם רואים זה
ממהרים לסור מעבודת הבורא וחשים להתרצות אל אנשי הרשע וללמד
ממעשיהם ויתברר הנבר לאלהים ויראה הנאמן בעבודתו בסבלו עת
ששולטין בו ומבישין אותו ויקבל שכר מהבורא יתעלה על זה כמו
שידעת מענין אליהו עם איזבל וירמיהו עם מלכי דורו.

וכיון שהתברר חיוב הגלגול על הסבות על בני אדם נבאר עתה כי אין כל
אדם חיב לחזר על כל סבה מסבות הטרף כי הסבות רבות.

מהן נקלות שטרחן מעט כסחורה בחנות או מלאכת יד שטרחה מעט
כתפירה וכאחוי והספרות ואצור המסחרים ושכיר האריסים והפועלים
והשמשים בעבודת האדמה.

16

ומהן סבות יש בהן יגיעה וטרח כעבוד העורות והוצאת הברזל והנחשת והעופרת מן מוצאיהם וזקוק הכסף בעופרת ונשא המשאות הכבדות ולכת בדרכים רחוקים תמיד ועבודת האדמה וחרישתה וכיוצא בהם.

ומי שהוא מבני אדם חזק בגופו וחלש בהכרתו ראוי לו מהן מה שיש בו מן היגיעה כפי שיכול לסבול

ומי שהוא חלש בגופו והכרתו חזקה אל יבקש מסבות הטרף מה שמיגע גופו אך יטה אל מה שיהיה קל על גופו ויוכל להתמיד עליו.

ולכל אדם יש חפץ במלאכה או סחורה מבלתי זולתה כבר הטביע האל לה בטבעו אהבה וחבה וכן בשאר החיים כמו שהטביע בטבע החתול צידת העכברים ובטבע הנץ צידת מה שראוי לו מן העוף ובטבע האיל צידת הנחשים. וכן יש מן העופות שיצודו הדגים לבד וכן בטבע מין ומין ממיני החיים נטיה ותאוה אל מין ממיני הצמחים והחיים הטבע עליו להיות סבה למזונו ותכנת גופו ואבריו ראויין לדבר ההוא כפה הארך והשוק הארך לעוף שהוא צד את הדגים וכשן והצפרן החזק לארי והקרנים לשור ולאיל ואשר תוכן מזונו מן הצמח לא נתן לו כלי הציד והטרף.

ועל הדמיון הזה תמצא מדות בני אדם וגופותם מוכנות לסחורות ולמלאכות. ומי שמוצא במדותיו וטבעו כסף אל מלאכה מהמלאכות ויהיה גופו ראוי לה ויוכל לסבל את טרחה יחזר עליה וישים אותה סבה להבאת מזונו ויסבל ויסבל מתקה ומרירותה ואל יקוץ כשימנע ממנו הטרף בקצת העתים אך יבטח באלהים שיספיק לו טרפו כל ימי חייו. ויכון בטרדת לבו וגופו בסבה מן הסבות והסבוב עליה לעמד במצות הבורא שצוה האדם להתעסק בסבות העולם כעבודת האדמה וחרישתה וזריעתה כמו שכתוב (בראשית ב טו) ויקח ה' אלהים את האדם ויניחהו בגן עדן לעבדה ולשמרה, ולהשתמש בשאר בעלי חיים בתועלותיו ומזוניו ובנין המדינות והכנת המזונות ולהשתמש בנשים ולבעל אותן להרבות הזרע

ויהיה נשכר על כונתו על בהם לאלהים בלבו ומצפונו בין שיגמר לו חפצו בין שלא יגמר לו חפצו כמו שכתוב (תהלים קכח ב) יגיע כפיך כי תאכל אשריך וטוב לך, ואמרו רבותינו זכרונם לברכה (משנה אבות ב יב) וכל מעשיך יהיו לשם שמים.

ויהיה בטחונו באלהים שלם ולא יזיקנו הסבוב על הסבות להבאת טרפו

בהם מאומה כשהוא מכון בהם בלבו ומצפונו לשם שמים.

ואל יחשב כי טרפו מעמד על סבה ידועה ושאם תמנע הסבה ההיא ממנו לא יבא בסבה אחרת אבל יבטח על האלהים בטרפו וידע כי הסבות כלן אצל הבורא שוות יטריפהו במה שירצה מהן ובעת שירצה מאיזה ענין שירצה כמו שאמר הכתוב (שמואל א יד ו) כי אין לה' מעצור להושיע ברב או במעט, ואמר (דברים ח יח) כי הוא הנותן לך כח לעשות חיל, ואמר (זכריה ד ו) לא בחיל ולא בכח כי אם ברוחי אמר ה' צבאות.

~~ פרק ד ~~
אבל הדברים שחיב המאמין לבטח בהם על הבורא יתעלה כוללים אותם שני מינים. אחד מהם דברי העולם הזה והשני דברי העולם הבא. ודברי העולם הזה יחלקו לשני חלקים.

אחד מהם עניני העולם לתועלות העולם הזה השני עניני העולם לתועלות העולם הבא.

ועניני העולם לתועלות העולם הזה יחלקו לשלשה חלקים.

אחד מהם תועלות גופו בלבד

והשני תועלות טרפו וסבות הונו ומיני קניניו

והשלישי תועלות בני ביתו ואשתו וקרוביו ואוהביו ואויביו ומי שהוא למעלה ממנו ולמטה ממנו מכתות בני אדם.

ועניני העולם לתועלות העולם הבא יחלקו לשני חלקים.

אחד מהם חובות הלבבות והאברים שהוא מתיחד בהם לבדו ואין מעשהו יוצא בהם להנאת זולתו ולא להזקו

והחלק השני חובות האברים אשר לא יוכל לעשותם אלא בהשתתפות זולתו עמו בפעל ובהפעל כצדקה וגמילות חסדים ולמוד החכמה ולצוות בטוב ולהזהיר מן הרע.

ועניני העולם הבא יחלקו לשני חלקים.

אחד מהם הגמול הראוי

והשני שהוא מחסד הבורא יתעלה על החסידים והנביאים לעולם הבא.
והנה כל הדברים שבוטחים בהם על הבורא יתברך שבעה חלקים.

אחד מהם עניני גוף האדם בלבד

והשני עניני הונו וסבות טרפו

והשלישי עניני אשתו ובניו וקרוביו ואוהביו ואויביו

והרביעי חובות הלבבות והאברים שהוא מתיחד בתועלותן והזקתן

והחמישי חובות האברים שתועלתן והזקתן מתעברות אל זולתו

והששי גמול העולם הבא אשר יהיה כפי המעשה בעולם הזה

והשביעי גמול העולם הבא אשר יהיה מהבורא יתברך על דרך החסד
על סגלתו ואוהביו כמו שכתוב (תהלים לא כ) מה רב טובך אשר צפנת
ליראיך פעלת לחוסים בך נגד בני אדם.

וכיון שפרשתי ההקדמות אשר בעבורן יתכן הבטחון מן הבוטח באלהים
יתעלה יש עלי לסמך להן פרוש אפני ישר הבטחון בכל אחד מהשבעה
דברים אשר בהם יבטח כל בוטח על אלהים ועל זולתו אחד אחד.

ואמר בפרוש החלק הראשון מהם והוא בעניני גוף האדם בלבד והם
חייו ומותו וטרף מזונו למחיתו ומלבושו ודירתו ובריאותו וחליו ומדותיו.
ואפני היושר בבטחון על אלהים בכל ענין מהם שישליך את נפשו בהם
להליכות הגזר אשר גזר לו הבורא מהם ותבטח נפשו באלהים יתברך
וידע כי לא יגמר לו מהם אלא מה שקדם בדעת הבורא שהוא הנכון
לעניניו בעולם הזה ובעולם הבא ויותר טוב לאחריתו ושהנהגת הבורא
לו בכלם שוה אין לשום בריה בהם עצה ולא הנהגה אלא ברשותו
וגזרתו ודינו.

וכמו שאין ביד הברואים חייו ומותו וחליו ובריאותו כן אין בידם טרף
מזונו וספוקו ולבושו ושאר עניני גופו.

ועם ברור אמונתו כי עניננו מסור אל גזרות הבורא יתעלה ושבחירת
הבורא לו היא הבחירה הטובה הוא חייב להתגלגל לסבות תועלותיו

19

ולבחר הטוב כנראה לו מן הענין והאלהים יעשה מה שקדמה בו גזרתו.

והדומה לזה כי אדם אף על פי שקצו ומדת ימיו קשורים בגזרת הבורא יתברך יש על האדם להתגלגל לסבות החיים במאכל ובמשתה ומלבוש ובמעון כפי צרכו ולא יניח את זה על האלהים שיאמר אם קדם בגזרת הבורא שאחיה ישאיר נפשי בגופי מבלי מזון כל ימי חיי ולא אטרח בבקשת הטרף ועמלו.

וכן אין ראוי לאדם להכנס בסכנות בבטחונו על גזרת הבורא וישתה סמי המות או שיסכן בעצמו להלחם עם הארי והחיות הרעות ללא דחק או שישליך עצמו בים או באש והדומה לזה ממה שאין האדם בטוח בהן ויסכן בנפשו. וכבר הזהירנו הכתוב מזה במה שאמר (דברים ו טז) לא תנסו את ה' אלהיכם וגו' כי איננו נמלט בזה מאחד משני דברים.

או שימות ויהיה הוא הממית את עצמו והוא נתבע על זה כאלו המית זולתו מבני אדם אף על פי שמותו על הדרך ההוא בגזרת האלהים וברשותו.

וכבר הזהירנו שלא להמית שום אדם בשום גלגול באמרו (שמות כ יג) לא תרצח וכל אשר יהיה המומת קרוב אל הממית יהיה העונש יותר ראוי כמו שכתוב (עמוס א יא) על רדפו בחרב אחיו ושחת רחמיו וגו'. וכן מי שהמית את עצמו יהיה ענשו גדול בלי ספק

מפני שמשלו בזה כעבד שצוהו אדוניו לשמר מקום לזמן ידוע והזהירו שלא יפרד ממנו עד שיבא שליח אדוניו אליו. וכן שראה שבושש השליח לבא נפרד מן המקום קדם בואו וקצף עליו אדוניו והענישו ענש גדול. וכן הממית את עצמו יוצא מעבודת האלהים אל המרותו בהכנסו בסכנת המות.

ועל כן אתה מוצא שמואל עליו השלום אומר (שמואל א טז ב) איך אלך ושמע שאול והרגני ולא נחשב לו לחסרון בבטחונו על האלהים אך היתה התשובה מאלהים לו במה שמורה על זריזותו בזה משבחת ואמר לו (שמואל א טז ב) עגלת בקר תקח בידך ואמרת לזבח לה' באתי ושאר הענין. ואילו היה זה קצור בבטחונו היתה התשובה אליו (דברים לב לט) אני אמית ואחיה וגו' או הדומה לו כמו שאמר למשה עליו השלום עת שאמר לו (שמות ד י) כי כבד פה וכבד לשון אנכי (שמות ד יא) מי שם פה לאדם וגו'. ואם שמואל עם תם צדקתו לא הקל להכנס בסבה קטנה מסבות הסכנה אף על פי שהיה נכנס בה במצות הבורא יתברך כשאמר

(שמואל א טז א) מלא קרנך שמן ולך אשלחך אל ישי בית הלחמי כל שכן שיהיה זה מגנה מזולתו מבלתי מצות הבורא יתעלה.

או שינצל בעזרת הבורא יתברך לו ויאבדו זכיותיו ויפסיד שכרו כמו שאמרו רבותינו זכרונם לברכה בזה הענין (גמרא שבת לב א) לעולם אל יעמד אדם במקום סכנה ויאמר שעושין לו נס שמא אין עושין לו נס ואם עושין לו נס מנכין לו מזכיותיו ואמר יעקב אבינו עליו השלום (בראשית לב יא) קטנתי מכל החסדים וגו' ואמר המתרגם בפרושו זעירין זכוותי מכל חסדין ומכל טבוון.

וכמו שאמרנו בחיים ובמות כן נאמר בחיוב תביעת סבות הבריאות והמזון והמלבוש והדירה והמדות הטובות ולהרחיק שכנגדן עם ברור אמונתו כי הסבות אין מועילות אותו בזה כלום אלא בגזרת הבורא יתברך כאשר יש לבעל האדמה לחרש אותה ולנקותה מן הקוצים ולזרעה ולהשקותה אם יזדמנו לו מים ויבטח על הבורא יתברך להפרותה ולשמרה מן הפגעים ותרבה תבואתה ויברך אותה הבורא ואין ראוי לו להניח האדמה מבלי עבודה וזריעה בבטחונו על גזרת הבורא שתצמיח האדמה בלתי זרע שקדם לו.

וכן בעלי המלאכה והסחורה והשכירות מצוין לחזר על הטרף בהם עם הבטחון באלהים כי הטרף בידו ורשותו ושהוא ערב בו לאדם ומשלימו לו באיזו סבה שירצה ואל יחשב כי הסבה תועילהו או תזיקהו מאומה.

ואם יבוא לו טרפו על פנים מאפני הסבות אשר התעסק בהן ראוי לו שלא יבטח על הסבה ההיא וישמח בה ויוסיף להחזיק בה ויטה לבו אליה כי יחלש בטחונו באלהיו. אך אין ראוי לו לחשב כי תועילנו יותר ממה שקדם בדעת הבורא ואל ישמח בהדבקו בה וסבובו עליה אך יודה הבורא אשר הטריפו אחר יגעתו ולא שם עמלו וטרחו לריק כמו שכתוב (תהלים קכח ב) יגיע כפיך כי תאכל אשריך וטוב לך.

ואמר אחד מן החסידים אני תמה ממי שנותן לחברו מה שגזר לו אצלו הבורא ואחר כך יזכיר לו טובתו עליו בו ויבקש להודות אותו עליו. ויותר אני תמה ממי שקבל טרפו על ידי אחר מכרח לתתו לו ויכנע לו ויפיסהו וישבחהו.

ואם לא יבואהו הטרף על הפנים אשר סבב עליהם אפשר שטרף יומו כבר קדם אצלו והוא ברשותו או שבא לו על פנים אחרים.

ועל איזה פנים שיהיה ראוי לו להתעסק בסבות ואל ירפה מחזר עליהן
כשהם ראויות למדותיו ולגופו ולאמונתו ולעולמו כאשר קדמתי ויבטח
עם זה על אלהיו שלא יעזבהו ולא ירפהו ולא יתעלם ממנו כמו שנאמר
(נחום א ז) טוב ה' למעוז ביום צרה וגו'.

וכן נאמר בענין הבריאות והחלי כי על האדם לבטח בבורא בזה
ולהשתדל בהתמדת הבריאות בסבות אשר מטבען זה ולדחות המדוה
במה שנהגו לדחותו כמו שצוה הבורא יתעלה (שמות כא יט) ורפא ירפא
מבלי שיבטח על סבות הבריאות והחלי שהן מועילות או מזיקות אלא
ברשות הבורא.

וכאשר יבטח בבורא ירפאהו מחליו בסבה ובלתי סבה כמו שנאמר
(תהלים קז כ) ישלח דברו וירפאם וגו'

ואפשר שירפאהו בדבר המזיק הרבה כמו שידעת מענין אלישע במים
הרעים שרפא הזקם במלח כמו שכתוב (מלכים ב ב יט) והמים רעים
והארץ משכלת, שריפא היזקם במלח, וכן (שמות טו כה) ויורהו ה' עץ
וישלך אל המים, ואמרו הקדמונים (במדרש תנחומא שם) שהיה עץ של
הרדופני וכמוהו (ישעיה לח כא) ישאו דבלת תאנים וימרחו על השחין ויחי
וכבר ידעת מה שהיה מענין אסא כשבטח על הרופאים והניח בטחונו
באלהים בחליו מהמוסר והתוכחה לו ואמר הכתוב (איוב ה יח) כי הוא
יכאיב ויחבש וגו'.

ופרוש החלק השני והוא ענייני קניני האדם וסבות טרפו ואפני עסקיו
במסחר ומלאכה והליכות הדרכים ומנוי ושכירות ופקידות ועבודת
המלכים וגזברות וקבלנות ואמנה וספרות ומיני העבודות והליכות
המדברות והימים והדומה לזה ממה שמתעסקין בו לקבץ ממון ולהרבות
מותרי המחיה אפני ישר הבטחון בהם על האלהים שיתעסק במה
שזימן לו הבורא מהם לצרך ספוקו ומזונו ולהגיע אל מה שיש בו די מן
העולם.

ואם יגזר לו הבורא בתוספת על זה תבואהו מבלי טרח ויגיעה כאשר
יבטח על האלהים בה ולא ירבה לחזר על הסבות ולא יסמך עליהן
בלבו.

ואם לא יגזרו לו יותר מן המזון אם היו משתדלים כל אשר בשמים
ובארץ להוסיף עליו לא היו יכולים בשום פנים ולא בשום סבה. וכאשר
יבטח באלהים ימצא מנוחת לבו ושלות נפשו כי לא יעברונו חקו אל

זולתו ולא יקדים ולא יאחר מעתו הנגזר לו בו.

ויש שמנהיג הבורא טרפי רבים מבני אדם על יד איש אחד מהם להבחין בזה עבודתו לאלהים מהמרותו ויישם את זה מן הסבות החזקות שבסבות הנסיון וההסתרה לו כמלך שהוא מטריף חילו ועבדיו וכן השרים ורואי המלך והסגנים אשר סביבותיהם כתות מעבדיהם ושמשיהם ופקידיהם ונשים וקרובים ומשתדלים בעבורם לחזר על סבת קבוץ הממון מפנים טובים ורעים.

והסכל מהם יטעה בשלשה פנים.

אחד מהם בקבצו הממון כי הוא לוקח מה שגזר לו הבורא לקחתו על פנים מגנים ורעים. ואלו היה מבקש אותו על אפניו היה מגיע אל חפצו ורצונו והיה מתקיים בידו ענין תורתו ועולמו ולא היה חסר לו ממה שגזר הבורא מאומה.

והשני כי הוא חושב שכל מה שהגיע אליו מן הממון הוא טרף מזונו ולא יבין כי הטרף מתחלק לשלשה חלקים אחד מהם טרף מזונו והוא כללת גופו בלבד והוא המבטח מן האלהים לכל אשר בו רוח חיים עד תכלית ימיו. והשני טרף מזון זולתו מאשה ובנים ועבדים ומשרתים והדומה להם ואיננו מבטח מן האלהים לכל הברואים אלא לסגלה מהם בתנאים מיחדים והוא מקרה מזדמן בעת אחת ואין מזדמן בעת אחרת כפי שמחיבות הליכות דיני הבורא מן החסד והמשפט. והשלישי טרף קנין והוא הממון אשר אין בו תועלת לאדם והוא שומר עליו ונוצר אותו עד אשר יורישנו לזולתו או שיאבד ממנו. והסכל יחשב כל אשר גזר לו הבורא מן הממון שהוא טרף מזונו וכללת גופו והוא ממהר אליו ומשתדל עליו ואפשר שיקבצנו לבעל אשתו אחריו ולהורגו ולגדול שבשונאיו.

והשלישי שהוא נותן הטרפים לבעליהם כמו שגזר להם הבורא על ידו והוא זוכר טובתו להם בהם כאלו הוא הטריפם בהם וכלכל אותם והתחסד בם עליהם ורוצה שיודוהו וישבחוהו הרבה עליהם ושיעבדוהו בעבורם ויתגאה ויגבה וירום לבבו ויניח הודאתו עליהם ויחשב שאם היה מונע אותם מהם היו נשארים אצלו וכי לולא הוא היו נפסקים טרפיהם. והוא העני אשר ייגע לריק בעולם הזה ויפסיד שכרו לעולם הבא.

והמשכיל נוהג בשלשת הפנים על הדרך הנכונה לתורתו ולעולמו

ובטחונו במה שיש ביד האלהים מטרפו וקנינו יותר חזק מבטחונו במה שיש בידו מהם מפני שאינו יודע אם הוא טרף מזון או טרף קנין ויגיע לכבוד העולם הזה ואל הגמול הטוב בעולם הבא כמו שנאמר במזמור (תהלים קיב א) הללויה אשרי איש ירא את ה' עד סופו.

ויש מבני אדם כתות שאינם משתדלים לקנות הממון ולהרבות ממנו אלא לאהבת הכבוד מבני אדם ולעשות להם שם ואין מספיק להם ממנו שום דבר וזה סכלות מהם בסבת הכבוד בעולם הזה ובעולם הבא. וגורם להם זה מה שרואים מכבוד עמי הארץ לאנשי הממון וכבודם להם לחמדם מה שיש אצלם ולמשך מאשר בידם.

ואלו השכילו והבינו כי אין ביכלתם ולא בכחם לא לתת ולא למנע אלא למי שגזר לו הבורא אצלם לא היו מקוים לזולתו

ולא היה ראוי אצלם לכבוד אלא מי שיחדהו הבורא במעלות משבחות ראוי בעבורן לכבוד הבורא יתעלה כמו שכתוב (שמואל א ב ל) כי מכבדי אכבד.

ומפני שסכלו עמי הארץ בכבדם בעלי הממון בסבות הכבוד הוסיף להם הבורא סכלות בסבות בקשותם ונפלו בהשתדלות גדולה ויגיעה רבה כל ימיהם והניחו מה שהיו חייבין להשתדל בו ולמהר אליו מהשלים חובות הבורא אשר עליהם ולהודות על טובותיו אצלם ותהיינה בקשותם יותר קרובות אליהם בדרך הזה בלי ספק כמו שאמר הכתוב (משלי ג טז) אורך ימים בימינה בשמאלה עושר וכבוד ואמר (דברי הימים א כט יב) והעושר והכבוד מלפניך וגו'.

ויש שימצא בכלל מבקשי הממון מי שיגיע ממנו אל תכלית תאותו בדרך הסבות אשר זכרנו ומהם מי שיגיע אליו בדרך הירשה והדומה לזה ויחשב כי הסבות חיבו לו את זה ולולא הן לא היה מגיע אליו ממנו כלום ומשבח הסבה מבלעדי המסבב.

וכמה הוא דומה בזה לאדם שהוא במדבר הכביד עליו הצמא ומצא מים שאינם מתוקים בבור אחד ושמח בהם שמחה גדולה ורוה מהם. וכאשר הלך מעט ומצא מעין נובע מים מתוקים דאג על מה שקדם משתותו המים הראשונים ורוותו מהם.

וכן בעל הממון שהגיע אליו בסבה ידועה אלו היתה נמנעת הסבה ההיא

ממנו היה משיג אותו בסבה אחרת כאשר הקדמנו וכמו שאמר (שמואל א
יד ו) כי אין לה' מעצור להושיע ברב או במעט.

וממה שראוי לבטוח על האלהים בטרפו כשיתעכב ממנו הטרף יום מן
הימים שיאמר בלבו כי אשר הוציאני אל העולם הזה בזמן ידוע ועת
ידועה ולא הוציאני אליו לפניהם ולא לאחריהם הוא שמעכב ממני בו
טרפי לעת ידוע ויום ידוע לדעתו מה שהוא טוב לי.

וכן כאשר יבואהו טרפו מצמצם לא יותר על מזונו מאומה ראוי לו לחשוב
בלבו ולומר אשר הכין לי מזוני בשדי אמי בתחלת עניני כפי צרכי ודי
כלכלתי יום יום עד אשר המיר אותו לי בטוב ממנו ולא הזיק לי בואו
בצמצום מאומה כן לא יזיק לי בוא הטרף הזה אשר העתיק אותי אליו
עתה בצמצום כפי צרכי עד תכלית ימי מאומה.

ויהיה נשכר על זה כמו שאמר הבורא על אבותינו במדבר שענינם היה
כזה (שמות טז ד) ויצא העם ולקטו דבר יום ביומו ואמר (ירמיה ב ב) הלוך
וקראת באזני ירושלים וגו'.

וכן אם יבואהו טרפו בסבה מבלי סבה ומקום מבלי מקום ועל ידי איש
מבלתי איש אחר יאמר בלבו אשר יצרני על צורה ותבנית ותכונה ומדה
מבלי שאר הצורות והתכונות והמדות לתקנת עניני הוא בחר לי שיבוא
טרפי על הפנים המפיקים לעניני מבלי שאר הפנים. ואשר הוציאני אל
העולם הזה במקום ידוע ועל ידי שני אישים ידועים מבלי שאר אישי
העולם הוא בחר לי בו טרפי בארץ ידועה ועל ידי איש ידוע שם אותו
סבה לטרפי לטוב לי כמו שאמר הכתוב (תהלים קמה יז) צדיק ה' בכל
דרכיו.

אבל פרוש החלק השלישי והם עניני אשתו ובניו ובני ביתו וקרוביו
ואוהביו ואויביו ומידעיו ומכיריו ואשר למעלה ממנו ואשר למטה ממנו
מכתות בני אדם אפני ישר הבטחון על האלהים בהם כאשר אספר והוא
שאין אדם נמלט מאחד משני דברים. שיהיה נכרי או שיהיה בתוך
משפחתו וקרוביו. ואם יהיה נכרי יהיה צוותו באלהיו בעת השתוממותו
ויבטח עליו בגרותו. ויעלה על לבו גרות הנפש בעולם הזה וכי אנשי
הארץ כמו גרים בה כמו שאמר הכתוב (ויקרא כה כג) כי גרים ותושבים
אתם עמדי. ויחשב בלבו כי כל מי שיש לו קרובים בו עד זמן מעט ישוב
נכרי בודד ולא יועילהו קרוב ולא בן ולא יתחבר עמו אחד מהם.

ויחשב אחר כך בהסתלקות כבד משאם וחובותם וצרכיהם מעליו ויחשב

זה טובה מטובות הבורא עליו מפני שאם יהיה רודף אחר עניני העולם
וצרכיו תהיה יגיעתו יותר קלה עליו מבלי אשה ובנים וחסרונם מנוחה לו
וטובה. ואם יהיה מבקש עניני אחריתו יהיה לבו יותר רק ופנוי בעת
התבודדותו מבלי ספק.

ועל כן היו הפרושים בורחים מקרוביהם ומבתיהם אל ההרים כדי שיפנו
לבותם לעבודת אלהים. וכן היו הנביאים בזמן הנבואה יוצאים
ממעונותיהם ומתבודדים לחובות הבורא עליהם כמו שידעת מענין
אליהו עם אלישע שנאמר עליו (מלכים א יט יט) שנים עשר צמדים לפניו
והוא בשנים העשר. וכיון שרמז לו אליהו במעט רמז הבין אותו ואמר
(מלכים א יט כ) אשקה נא לאבי ולאמי ואלכה אחריך, ואמר (מלכים א יט כא)
וילך אחרי אליהו וישרתהו.

ואמרו על אחד מהפרושים שנכנס למדינה אחת להורות את יושביה
עבודת האלהים וימצאם לובשים צבע אחד במלבושיהם ותכשיטיהם
וראה קבריהם אצל פתחי בתיהם ולא ראה בינהם אשה. ושאל אותם
על זה ואמרו לו מה שאנו לובשים צבע אחד שלא יהיה נכר העני מן
העשיר ושלא יבא העשיר להתגאות ולהתפאר בעשרו ויבא העני
להתבזות אצל עצמו ושידמה ענינינו על האדמה ענינינו תחתיה. ונאמר
על אחד מהמלכים שהיה מתערב בין עבדיו ולא היה נכר בינהם מפני
שהיה נוהג מנהג השפלות בתכשיטיו ובמלבושיו.

ומה ששמענו קברות מתינו אצל פתחינו כדי שנוכח מהם ונהיה נכונים
למות ונזמין לנו הצדה המגעת אותנו למקום המנוחה. ומה שראית
שפרשנו מן הנשים והבנים דע כי יחדנו להם קריה קרובה מכאן
כשיצטרך אחד ממנו על דבר מדבריהם ילך אליהם וישלים צרכו וישוב
אלינו מפני שראינו במה שיכנס עלינו מטרדת הלב ורב ההפסד וגדל
היגיעה והטרח בקרבתם והמנוחה מכל זה בהרחקתם לבחר בעניני
העולם הבא ולמאס בעניני העולם הזה. וייטבו דבריהם בעיני הפרוש
ויברך אותם ויאשרם בענינם.

ואם יהיה הבוטח באלהים בעל אשה וקרובים ואוהבים ואויבים יבטח
באלהים בהצלתו מהם

וישתדל לפרע מה שחיב להם ולעשות חפציהם ולהיות לבו שלם עמהם
וירף ידו מהזקתם ויסבב על מה שיהיה טוב להם ויהיה נאמן בכל
עניניהם ויורם אפני תועלותם בעניני התורה והעולם לעבודת הבורא
כמו שכתוב (ויקרא יט יח) ואהבת לרעך כמוך, ואמר (ויקרא יט יז) לא תשנא

את אחיך בלבבך לא ליחל הגמול מהם ולא לקדם אצלם ולא מאהבתו
בכבודם ושבחם ולא להשתרר עליהם אך לקיים מצות הבורא ולשמור
בריתו ופקודיו עליהם.

כי מי שתהיה דעתו בעשותו חפציהם על אחד מהדברים שזכרנו תחלה
לא ישיג רצונו מהם בעולם הזה וייגע לריק ויפסיד שכרו לעולם הבא.
ואם הוא נוהג בזה לעבודת האלהים בלבד יעזרם האלהים לגמל אותו
בעולם הזה וישים בפיהם שבחו ויגדל ענינו בעיניהם ויגיע אל הגמול
הגדול בעולם הבא כמו שאמר האלהים לשלמה (מלכים א ג יג) וגם אשר
לא שאלת נתתי לך וגו'.

אבל אפני בטחונו על אלהיו בעניני מי שהוא למעלה ממנו ומי שהוא
למטה ממנו מכתות בני אדם הפנים הישרים לו כשיביא אותו הצרך
לבקש חפץ ממי שהוא למעלה ממנו או למטה ממנו שיבטח בו על
אלהיו וישימם סבה בהשלמתו כאשר ישים עובדת הארץ וזריעתה סבה
לטרפו. ואם ירצה להטריפו ממנה יצמח הזרע ויפרה וירבה ואין להודות
הארץ על זה אך ההודאה לבורא לבדו. ואם לא יחפץ האלהים להטריפו
ממנו לא תצמיח הארץ או תצמיח ויקרה הצמח פגע ואין להאשים
הארץ.

וכן כשיבקש מאחד מהם חפץ שיהיה אצלו החלש והחזק מהם שוה
בעשותו ויבטח בהשלמתו על האלהים יתברך.

ואם ישלם על ידי אחד מהם יודה הבורא יתברך אשר השלים חפצו
ויודה למי שנעשה על ידו על לבו על הטוב לו ושהבורא הביא תועלתו על
ידו. ובידוע שאין הבורא מגלגל טובה אלא על ידי הצדיקים ומעט הוא
שמתגלגל הפסד על ידיהם כמו שאמרו חכמינו זכרונם לברכה (גמרא
בבא בתרא קיט ב) מגלגלין זכות ע"י זכאי וחובה ע"י חייב, ואמר הכתוב
(משלי יב כא) לא יאונה לצדיק כל און.

ואם לא ישלם לו על ידיהם אל יאשימם ואל יתלה בהם הקצר אך יודה
לאלהים אשר בחר לו הטוב בזה וישבחם כפי שידע מהשתדללם לעשות
חפצו אף על פי שלא נשלם כרצונו וכרצונם לו. וכן ינהג במידעיו ואוהביו
ובמי שנושא ונותן עמהם ושמשיו ושתפיו.

וכן אם יבקש ממנו מי שלמעלה ממנו או שלמטה ממנו חפץ יסבב
לעשותו בכל לבו וישתדל להשלימו במצפונו אם יזדמן לו ויהיה מי
שמבקשו ראוי להשתדל לו בו ואחר כך יבטח על האלהים בהשלמתו.

27

ואם ישלימהו על ידו וישימהו סבה לטובת זולתו יודה על זה. ואם ימנע
ממנו ולא יזדמן לו לעשותו אל יאשים נפשו ויודיע את חברו שלא קצר
אחר שיטרח וישתדל בו בעצמו. אבל עניני אויביו וחומדיו ומבקשי רעתו
יבטח בעניניהם על הבורא יתעלה ויסבל חרפתם ואל יגמל להם כפעלם

אך יגמלם חסד ויעשה להם כל מה שיוכל לעשותו מן הטוב ויזכר בלבו
שתועלתו ונזקו ביד הבורא יתעלה.

ואם יהיו סבה להזיקו יחשב עליהם טוב ויחשד את עצמו ומעשיו ברע
הקדמותיו אצל אלהיו ויתחנן אל האלהים ויבקש מלפניו לכפר עונותיו
ואז ישובו אויביו לאהבתו כמו שאמר החכם (משלי טז ז) ברצות ה׳ דרכי
איש גם אויביו ישלים אתו.

ופרוש החלק הרביעי בעניני חובות הלבבות והאברים שהאדם מתיחד
בתועלותם ונזקם וזה כצום וכתפלה וכסכה וכלולב וכציצית ושמירת
השבת והמועדים והמנע מן העברות וכל חובות הלבבות אשר לא
תעברנה אל זולתו ותועלותן ונזקן מיחדות בו מבלי שאר בני אדם אפני
ישר הבטחון בכלם על האלהים יתברך מה שאני מבאר אותו ומאלהים
אשאל להורות אותי האמת ברחמיו.

והוא כי מעשי העבודה והעברה לא יתכנו לאדם כי אם בהקבץ שלשה
דברים. האחד הבחירה בלבו ומצפונו והשני הכונה וההסכמה לעשות
מה שבחר בו והשלישי שישתדל לגמר המעשה באבריו הנראים
ויוציאהו אל גדר המעשה.

ומה שאינו נעלם ממנו בהם כבחירת העבודה והעברה והכונה
וההסכמה על המעשה הבטחון על האלהים בזה טעות וסכלות כי
הבורא יתברך הניח ברשותונו בחירת עבודתו והמרותו כמו שכתוב
(דברים ל׳ ט) ובחרת בחיים

ולא הניח ברשותונו השלמת המעשה בעבודה ובעברה אלא בסבות
שהם חוץ לנו מזדמנות בקצת העתים ונמנעות בקצתם

ואם יבטח על האלהים בבחירת עבודתו ויאמר לא אבחר ולא אכון
לעשות כלום מעבודת הבורא עד שיבחר לי הטוב ממנה כבר תעה
מדרך הישרה ומעדו רגליו מאפני הנכונה כי הבורא יתברך כבר צונו
לבחר במעשי העבודה ולכון אליה בהשתדלות והסכמה ובלב שלם
לשמו הגדול והודיענו שהוא אפני הנכונה לנו בעולם הזה ובעולם הבא.

28

ואם יזדמנו הסבות ויתכן גמר המעשה בעבודתו אשר קדמה בחירתנו
בה יהיה לנו השכר הגדול על הבחירה בעבודה ועל הכונה לעשותה ועל
השלמת מעשיה באברים הנראים. ואם ימנע מן האברים גמר המעשה
יהיה לנו שכר הבחירה והכונה כאשר זכרנו במה שקדם וכן העונש על
העברה.

וההפרש שבין עבודת הבורא ושאר מעשי העולם בענין הבטחון
באלהים יתברך שׁשאר עניני העולם לא נגלו לנו אפני הטוב והרע בסבה
מן הסבות מבלעדי שאריתם ולא אפני ההפסד והרע בקצתם בלתי
קצתם כי לא עמדנו על איזו מלאכה מן המלאכות שטובה לנו וויותר
ראויה לבקשת הטרף והבריאות והטוב ולא באיזו סחורה ובאיזו דרך
ובאיזה מעשה מן המעשים העולמיים נצליח כשנתגלגל בהם.

ומן הדין עלינו שנבטח באלהים בבחירתה והשלמתה לעזרנו על מה
שיש בו טובתנו אחר שנתגלגל עליהם ונתחנן אליו להעיר לבבנו
לבחירת הטובה והראויה לנו מהם.

אבל עבודת הבורא יתברך איננה כן מפני שכבר הודיענו אפני הנכונה
בה וצונו לבחר בה ונתן לנו היכלת עליה. ואם נתחנן אליו בבחירתה
ונבטח עליו בהראותנו אפני הטוב לנו נהיה תועים בדברינו וסכלים
בבטחוננו מפני שכבר קדמה הודעתו אותנו דרכי העבודה אשר יועילנו
בעולם הזה ובבא כמו שאמר (דברים ו כד) ויצונו ה' לעשות את כל החקים
האלה וגו' לטוב לנו כל הימים, ואמר בגמול העולם הבא (דברים ו כה)
וצדקה תהיה לנו כי נשמר לעשות.

ועוד כי עניני העולם יש שתשוב הסבה המשבחת מגנה והמגנה
משבחת אך העבודה והעברה אינם כן כי המגנה והמשבח מהם לא
יעתק מענינו ולא יתחלף לעולם.

אבל מה שראוי לבטח עליו הוא גמר מעשה העבודה אחר בחירתה בלב
שלם ונאמן והסכמה והשתדלות בבר לבב וכונה לשמו הגדול ובזה
אנחנו חיבין להתחנן אליו לעזר אותנו בו ולהורות אותנו עליו כמו שכתוב
(תהלים כה ה) הדריכני באמתך ולמדני, ואמר (תהלים קיט לה) הדריכני
בנתיב מצותיך וגו', ואמר (תהלים קיט ל) דרך אמונה בחרתי וגו', ואמר
(תהלים קיט לא) דבקתי בעדותיך ה' אל תבישני, ואמר (תהלים קיט מג) ואל
תצל מפי דבר אמת עד מאד וגו'.

29

וכל זה ראיה שבחירתו היתה במעשה העבודה אך התפלל אל האלהים על שני דברים.

אחד מהם ליחד לבבו ולחזק בחירתו בעבודתו בהרחקת טרדות העולם מלבו ועיניו כמו שאמר (תהלים פו יא) יחד לבבי ליראה שמך, (תהלים קיט יח) גל עיני ואביטה וגו', (תהלים קיט לז) העבר עיני וגו', (תהלים קיט לו) הט לבי אל עדותיך וגו', והדומה להם.

והשני לחזק אבריו על השלמת המעשים בעבודתו והוא מה שאמר (תהלים קיט לה) הדריכני בנתיב מצותיך, (תהלים קיט קיז)סעדני ואושעה, והרבה כמוהו. ואני עתיד לבאר אפני מפסידי החלק הזה ואפני השלמתו והדרך הנכונה בו בעזרת השם.

אבל פרוש החלק החמישי והוא חובות האברים אשר תועלתם ונזקם מתעברים אל זולתו כצדקה והמעשר ולמוד החכמה וצוות בטוב והזהר מהרע ולהשיב האמנות ולהסתיר הסוד ולדבר טוב ולעשות הטוב וכבוד אבות והשבת הרשעים אל האלהים והורות בני אדם דרכי טובתם ולחמל עניהם ולרחם עליהם ולסבל חרפתם כשמעיר אותם אל העבודה ומיחל אותם ומיראם בגמול ובענש.

אפני יושר הבטחון בזה שיהיה האדם צופן בלבבו כל המעשים האלה והדומה להם ויבחר עשותם ויסבב אליהם כפי מה שהקדמנו בחלק הרביעי מחיוב הבחירה עלינו להתקרב אל האלהים בלבד לא לקנות שם וכבוד ביניהם ולא לקוות הגמול מהם ולא להשתרר עליהם. ואחר כך יבטח על האלהים בהשלמת המעשה שכן לעשותו מהם כפי מה שהוא רוצה בו ממנו אחרי שיסבב עליו

ויזהר כפי יכלתו בכל זה להסתירו ממי שאין צריך לו להודיע כי בהיותו נסתר יהיה שכרו יותר גדול ממה שיהיה אם יהיה נודע. ומה שלא יוכל להסתירו יזכר בו השרש אשר הקדמנו כי התועלת והנזק לא יהיה מן הברואים כי אם ברשות הבורא יתברך.

וכאשר יגלגל הבורא על ידו מצוה יחשב בלבו כי הוא טובה מאת הבורא יתעלה שהטיב בה אליו ואל ישמח בשבח אותו בני אדם עליה ואל יחפץ בכבודם בעבורה ויביאהו זה להתגאות במעשהו ויפסיד לבו וכונתו לאלהים ויפסיד מעשהו ויאבד שכרו. ואני עתיד לבאר זה בשערו בעזרת השם.

אבל פרוש החלק הששי והוא בגמול העולם הזה והעולם הבא אשר יהיה האדם ראוי לו במעשה הטוב בעולם הוא שהגמול על שני פנים גמול בעולם הזה בלבד וגמול בעולם הבא בלבד. ויש שיהיו ראויים שניהם על מעשה אחד

ולא פרש לנו באור זה באר היטב. אך ערב הבורא לעמו גמול כולל על מעשה כולל ולא חלק הגמול על העבודות בעולם כמו שעשה בענש על העברות בעולם כמו שפרש המעשים שעושיהם חייבין סקילה שרפה הרג וחנק ומלקות ארבעים ומיתה וכרת ותשלומי כפל ותשלומי ארבעה וחמשה ונזק שור ובור ושן ואש ונותן מום באדם ושולחת יד במבשיו והמוציא שם רע והדומה לזה. אבל גמול העולם הבא וענשו לא פרש מהם הנביא מאומה בספרו בעבור כמה פנים.

מהם כי צורת הנפש בלעדי הגוף אינה ידועה אצלנו כל שכן מה שתתענג בו או תצטער בענין ההוא אך פרש אותו למי שהיה מבין הענין הזה כמו שאמר ליהושע (זכריה ג ז) ונתתי לך מהלכים בין העומדים האלה. ולא יהיה זה בעוד נפשו קשורה בגופו אבל רמז למה שיהיה אחר המות שתשוב הנפש בצורת המלאכים בענין פשיטותה ודקותה ועזבה להשתמש בגופה כשתתזדכך ותזהיר והיו מעשיה טובים בעולם הזה.

ומהם שגמול העולם הבא וענשו היה מקבל אצל עמי הארץ מהנביאים ומשכל אצל החכמים והניחו לזכרו בספר כמו שהניחו לזכר הרבה מפרוש המצות והחובות מפני שסמכו על הקבלה.

ומהם שהעם היו מן הסכלות ומעוט ההבנה בענין שאיננו נעלם ממה שכתוב בתורה.

ונהג הבורא עמהם מנהג האב החומל על בנו הקטן כשהוא רוצה ליסרו בנחת ולאט כמו שכתוב (הושע יא א) כי נער ישראל ואוהבהו. והאב כשרוצה ללמד את בנו בנערותו החכמות אשר יעלה בהם אל המעלות העליונות אשר לא יבינן הנער בעת ההיא אלו היה מפיס אותו עליהן ואומר לו סבל יגיעות המוסר והלמוד בעבור שתעלה בהן אל המעלות החמודות לא היה סובל את זה ולא שומע אליו מפני שאין מבין אותן.

וכאשר ייעדהו על זה במה שהוא ערב לו מיד ממאכל ומשתה ומלבוש נאה ומרכבת נאה והדומה לזה וייעידהו במה שיצער אותו מיד מרעב ועירם ומלקות והדומה להם וישב דעתו על מה שיבטח עליו מן הראיות

31

המרגשות והעדיות הגלויות האמתיות יקל עליו לסבל יגיעת המוסר ולשאת טרחו.

וכאשר יגיע לימי הבחרות ויחזק שכלו יבין הענין המכון אליו במוסרו ויכון אליו ותמעט בעיניו הערבות אשר היה רץ אליה בתחלת ענייניו והיה זה לחמלה עליו.

וכן הבורא יתברך יחל עמו והפחידם בגמול וענש ממהרים מפני שידע כי העם כאשר יתקנו לעבודה תגל מעליהם סכלותם בגמול העולם הבא וענשו ויכונו בעבודה אליו ויתנהגו בה עדיו וכן נאמר בכל מה שבספרים מהגשמת הבורא יתברך.

ומהם שגמול העולם הבא אין אדם ראוי לו במעשהו הטוב בלבד אך יהיה ראוי מן האלהים בשני דברים אחר המעשה הטוב. האחד שיורה בני האדם עבודת הבורא יתעלה וינהיגם לעשות הטוב כמו שכתוב (דניאל יב ג) ומצדיקי הרבים ככוכבים לעולם ועד, ואמר (משלי כד כה) ולמוכיחים ינעם ועליהם תבא ברכת טוב. וכאשר יתקבץ למשתדל גמול הצדקתו אל גמול צדקתו וגמול אמונת לבו וסבלו יהיה ראוי לגמול העולם הבא אצל הבורא.

והשני חסד מאלהים ונדבה וטובה כמו שכתוב (תהלים סב יג) ולך אדני חסד כי אתה תשלם לאיש כמעשהו.

והעלה בזה כי אם היה מעשה האדם כחול הים במספר לא יהיה שקול בטובה אחת מן טובות הבורא יתברך עליו בעולם הזה כל שכן אם יהיה לו חטא ואם ידקדק הבורא עם האדם בתביעת הודאת הטובה יהיה כל מעשהו נכחד ונשקע בקטנה שבטובות הבורא עליו. ומה שיהיה מגמול הבורא לו אינו מגיע לו על מעשהו אלא הוא מחסד הבורא עליו.

אך הענש בשני העולמים הוא באמת ובדין וחוב שחיב בו האדם אלא שחסד הבורא יתגבר עליו בשני העולמים כמו שכתוב (תהלים סב יג) ולך אדני חסד (תהלים עח לח) והוא רחום יכפר עון וגו'.

ומהם כי המעשה הטוב מתחלק לשני חלקים ממנו נסתר אין משקיף עליו זולת הבורא כחובות הלבבות והדומה להם

וממנו נראה על האברים איננו נסתר מן הברואים והם המצות הנראות על האברים.

והבורא יתברך גומל על המעשה הנראה על האברים בגמול נראה
בעולם הזה וגומל על המעשה הצפון והנסתר בגמול נסתר והוא גמול
העולם הבא. ועל כן זכרו דוד עליו השלום במלה שמורה על הענין כמו
שאמר (תהלים לא כ) מה רב טובך אשר צפנת ליראיך וגו' וכן דרך העונש
הנראה והנסתר כדרך הגמול.

והראיה על זה כי האל יתעלה ערב לעמו על העבודה הנראית על
האברים גמול נראה מהר בעולם הזה והוא המפרש בפרשת אם
בחקותי. וכן ערב להם על העבירות הנראות הגלויות ענש נראה מהר
בעולם הזה לפי שאין להמון העם אלא מה שנראה מהמעשים לא מה
שנסתר והוא מה שאמר (דברים כט כח) הנסתרות לה' אלהינו והנגלות
לנו ולבנינו עד עולם, ואמר הכתוב (ויקרא כ ד-ה) ואם העלם יעלימו עם
הארץ וגו' ושמתי אני את פני באיש ההוא וגו'. אך העבודות והעבירות
הצפונות בלב דין גמולם על הבורא יתברך בעולם הזה ובעולם הבא על
כן הניח הספר פרוש גמול העולם הבא.

ומהם כי הגמול והענש הנזכרים בספר דבר הנביא בגמול העולם הזה
וענשו לאנשי העולם ומפני שהיה יהושע בן יהוצדק בעולם המלאכים
אמר לו (זכריה ג ז) ונתתי לך מהלכים בין העומדים האלה, כי זה דרך
היחול וההפחדה שיהיה כראוי לזמן ולמקום ואתה הבן.

ומהם שגמול העולם הבא אין אין תכליתו אלא להדבק באלהים ולהתקרב
אל אורו העליון כמו שכתוב (ישעיה נח ח) והלך לפניך צדקך כבוד ה'
יאספך, ואמר (דניאל יב ג) והמשכילים יזהירו כזוהר הרקיע וגו', ואמר
(איוב לג ל) לאור באור החיים. ולא יגיע אליו אלא מי שרצה הבורא בו
ורצון הבורא שרש הגמול כמו שכתוב (תהלים ל ו) כי רגע באפו חיים
ברצונו, ואמר בפרשת אם בחקותי רמזים שמורים על הרצון מאלהים
והוא מה שאמר (ויקרא כו יא) ואמר (ויקרא כו ט) ולא תגעל נפשי אתכם,
ואמר (ויקרא כו י) ופניתי אליכם והייתי לכם לאלהים ואתם תהיו לי לעם.

והבטחון על האלהים במה שיעד בו הצדיקים מגמול העולם הזה
והעולם הבא על העבודה שישלמהו למי שראוי לו וכן ישלם העונש למי
שראוי לו מן הדין על המאמין ובטחונו על האלהים בזה מהשלמת
האמונה באלהים כמו שכתוב (בראשית טו ו) והאמין בה' ויחשבה לו
צדקה, ואמר (תהלים כז יג) לולא האמנתי לראות בטוב ה' בארץ חיים.

ואין ראוי לבטח על מעשהו הטוב ויבטיח נפשו בגמול העולם הזה

והעולם הבא על מעשהו אך יטרח וישתדל בהודאה לטובות הבורא התמידות עליו לא לתקות גמול עתיד שיתחיב לו במעשהו. אך יבטח על האלהים בו אחר ההשתדלות לפרע הודאת הבורא על גדל טובתו עליו כמו שאמרו רבותינו זכרונם לברכה (משנה אבות א ג) אל תהיו כעבדים המשמשים את הרב על מנת לקבל פרס אלא הוו כעבדים המשמשים את הרב שלא על מנת לקבל פרס ויהי מורא שמים עליכם.

והיה אחד מן החסידים אומר לא יגיע האדם אל גמול העולם הבא במעשהו אם מדקדקים עמו בחשבון במה שהוא חיב לאלהים על טובותיו עליו אבל בחסד האלהים עליו על כן אל תבטחו במעשיכם. ואמר דוד בזה (תהלים סב יג) ולך אדני חסד כי אתה תשלם לאיש כמעשהו.

אבל פרוש החלק השביעי והוא בחסד האלהים על בחיריו וסגלתו בעולם הבא ברוב הטובות אשר לא נוכל לספרן אפני ישר הבטחון על האלהים בו שיתעסק בסבות המגיעות אותו אל מדרגות החסידים הראוים לזה מאת האלהים יתברך בחסדו. והוא שינהג במדות אנשי הפרישות המואסים בעולם הזה ולהוציא אהבתו מלבו וימיר זה באהבת הבורא יתברך ולהמסר אליו ולהשתעשע בו ולהשתומם מהעולם ויושביו ויתנהג במנהגי הנביאים והחסידים ויהיה לבו בטוח באלהים שיתחסד עמו כמו שהתחסד עמם בעולם הבא.

אבל מי שיבטח על האלהים שיזכהו לזה מבלי מצוע מעשה הוא הכסיל הפתי והוא דומה למי שנאמר עליהם (גמרא סוטה כב ב) עושים מעשה זמרי ומבקשים שכר כפנחס. ומסמני אנשי המעלה הגדולה הזאת שיורו עבדי הבורא אל עבודת הבורא והסבל בעת הנסיון והצרה ושיקל בעיניהם כל דבר אצל קיום מצות הבורא יתברך כמו שידעת מן הענין (בראשית כב א) והאלהים נסה את אברהם, וענין חנניה מישאל ועזריה בכבשן האש (דניאל ג יג) ודניאל בגוב האריות (דניאל ו יג) ועשרה הרוגי מלכות.

ומי שבחר במות בעבודת הבורא מן החיים בהמרותו והריש מן העשר והחלי מן הבריאות והצרה מן השלוה ונמסר לדין הבורא ורצה בגזרתו ראוי הוא לחסד הבורא עליו ובנועם העולם הבא אשר אמר עליו הכתוב (משלי ח כא) להנחיל אהבי יש ואוצרותיהם אמלא, ואמר (ישעיה סד ג) עין לא ראתה אלהים זולתך יעשה למחכה לו, ואמר (תהלים לא כ) מה רב טובך אשר צפנת ליראיך.

34

~~ פרק ה ~~

אבל ההפרש שבין הבוטח על האלהים וזולתו בענין התעסקו בסבות הטרף אמר כי הבוטח באלהים יבהל מזולת הבוטח עליו בשבעה ענינים.

אחד מהם כי הבוטח באלהים רוצה בדינו בכל ענייניו ומודה לו על הטובה ועל הרעה כמו שאמר (איוב א כא) ה' נתן וה' לקח יהי שם ה' מבורך, וכמו שכתוב (תהלים קא א) חסד ומשפט אשירה, ואמרו רבותינו זכרונם לברכה (גמרא ברכות ס ב) אם חסד אשירה ואם משפט אשירה, ואמרו (משנה ברכות ט ה) חייב אדם לברך על הרעה כשם שמברך על הטובה.

ואשר איננו בוטח באלהים מתהלל על הטובה כמו שנאמר (תהלים י ג) כי הלל רשע על תאות נפשו וגו', ומתקצף באלהים על הרע כמו שנאמר (ישעיה ח כא) והיה כי ירעב והתקצף וקלל במלכו וגו'.

והשני כי הבוטח באלהים נפשו במנוחה ולבו שלו מצד הגזרות לדעתו כי הבורא ינהיגן לטובתו בעולמו ואחריתו כמו שאמר דוד עליו השלום (תהלים סב ו) אך לאלהים דומי נפשי כי ממנו תקותי. ואשר איננו בוטח באלהים הוא בצער תדיר ודאגה ארכה ואבל ועצב לא ימושו ממנו בטובה וברעה. בטובה מפני מעוט רצותו במצבו ושאיפתו להוסיף ולהרבות ולכנס. וברעה מפני שהוא קץ בה והיא כנגד תאותו וטבעו ומדותיו. וכן אמר החכם (משלי טו טו) כל ימי עני רעים וגו'.

והשלישי כי הבוטח באלהים ואם יתעסק בסבות לא יסמך בלבו עליהן ולא יקוה מהן תועלת ולא נזק מבלתי רצון האל אך מתעסק בהן לבחר בעבודת הבורא אשר צוה להתעסק בעולם לישבו ולזינו. ואם תגיעהו תועלת או ידחה בהן הנזק יודה האלהים לבדו על זה ולא יוסיף בהן אהבה וחבה יתרה ולא תנוח נפשו עליהן יותר אך יחזק בטחונו באלהים ויסמך לבו עליו מבלעדי הסבות. ואם לא יועילוהו הסבות ידע כי יבואהו טרף כשירצה יי מאיזה ענין שירצה ולא ימאס בהן בעבור זה ולא יניח להתעסק בהם לעבודת הבורא.

ואשר איננו בוטח באלהים מתעסק בסבות לבטחונו עליהן שהן מועילות אותו ודוחות הנזק מעליו. ואם הן מועילות אותו ישבח אותן וישבח השתדלותו בהן ויבחר אותן ולא יפנה אל זולתן. ואם אינן מועילות לו יניח אותן וימאסן וישוב חפצו מהן כמו שאמר הכתוב (חבקוק א טז) על כן יזבח לחרמו ויקטר למכמרתו.

35

והרביעי כי הבוטח באלהים כשיותר לו דבר על מזונו יוציאנו במה שמפיק רצון הבורא יתברך בנדיבות נפשו וטוב לבבו כמו שנאמר (דברי הימים א כט יד) כי ממך הכל וגו'.

ומי שאיננו בוטח באלהים איננו רואה העולם וכל אשר בו די פרנסתו וספוק צרכו והוא חס על ממונו מהשלים חובות הבורא וחובות בני אדם ממנו ואיננו מרגיש בו עד שיאבד ממנו ממונו וישאר זולתו כמו שאמר החכם (משלי יא כד) יש מפזר ונוסף עוד וחושך מיושר אך למחסור.

והחמישי כי הבוטח באלהים הוא מתעסק בסבות העולם להכין מהם צידה לאחריתו וספוק לבית מועדו ומה שיתברר לו בו הצלת תורתו ועולמו מתעסק בו ומה שיהיה בו שום הפסד בתורתו או מביא להמרות הבורא איננו מתעסק בו שלא יביא לעצמו מדוה תחת הארוכה.

ומי שאינו בוטח באלהים בוטח על הסבות ותנוח דעתו עליהן ולא ירחק מדבר מהן ויתעסק במשבח ובמגנה מהן ולא יחשב באחרית ענינו כמו שאמר החכם בהן (משלי יד טז) חכם ירא וסר מרע.

והששי כי הבוטח באלהים הוא אהוב לכל כתות בני אדם ודעתם נוחה עליו מפני שהם בטוחים מהזקתו ולבם שלם מחמתו ולא יפחדו ממנו על נשיהם ועל ממונם. והוא גם כן בטוח מהם מפני שיודע שתועלתו ונזקו אינם ביד נברא ולא ביכלתו ועל כן איננו מפחד מהזקתם כאשר איננו מקוה הנאתם. וכשהוא בטוח מהם והם בטוחים ממנו יאהבם ויאהבוהו כמו שכתוב (תהלים לב י) והבוטח בה' חסד יסובבנו.

ומי שאיננו בוטח באלהים אין לו אוהב מפני שהוא בכל עת חומד אותם ומקנא בם וחושב כל טובה שתגיע אליהם סרה ממנו ושטרפיהם לקוחים מטרפו וכל מה שנמנע ממנו מתאוותיו הוא בעבורם ובידם להגיעו אל תאוותיו. ואם תבואהו רעה או פגע בממונו ובניו יחשב כי הוא מאתם ושבידם להעביר הנזק ולדחות הרעה מעליו. וכיון שקדמו אלה ההקדמות בנפשו יבוא בעבור זה למאס אותם ולדבר בהם ולקללם ולשנא אותם והוא הנמאס בשני העולמים והמגנה בשני המעונים כמו שאמר הכתוב (משלי יז כ) עקש לב לא ימצא טוב.

והשביעי כי הבוטח באלהים לא יאבל בהמנע בקשה ולא בהפקד אהוב ולא יאצר הנמצא ואיננו חושש ליותר מטרף יומו כי לא יעלה על לבו מה יהיה למחרתו מפני שאיננו יודע עת בוא קצו ובוטח באלהים להאריך לו

בו ולהזמין טרפו ומזונו בו. ואיננו שמח בעתיד ולא יאבל לו כמו שאמר הכתוב (משלי כז א) אל תתהלל ביום מחר כי לא תדע מה ילד יום, ואמר בן סירא (גמרא סנהדרין ק ב) אל תצר צרת מחר כי לא תדע מה ילד יום, מחר יבא ואיננו ונמצא מצטער על עולם שאינו שלו. אבל דאגתו ואבלו על מה שהוא מקצר בו מחובות הבורא ומשתדל לפרוע מה שיוכל לפרוע מהם בנראהו ובנסתרו מפני שהוא חושב במיתתו ובוא יום האסיפה. ופחדו שיבואהו המות פתאם יוסיף לו השתדלות וזריזות להכין צידה לאחריתו ולא ירגיש על מה שיזמין לעולם הזה והוא מה שאמרו (משנה אבות ב י) שוב יום אחד לפני מיתתך ופרשו בו (גמרא שבת קנג א) ישוב היום שמא ימות למחר ונמצא כל ימיו בתשובה כדכתיב (קהלת ט ח) בכל עת יהיו בגדיך לבנים.

ואשר איננו בוטח באלהים ירבה אבלו להתמדת פגעי העולם עליו ויפקד אוהביו וימנעו ממנו בקשותיו ויזמין מהון העולם הרבה כאלו בטח מן החליפה וסרה מעליו אימת המות כאלו ימיו לא יתמו וחייו לא יכלו איננו זוכר אחריתו ומתעסק בעולמו איננו מעין בעניין תורתו וצידתו ובית מועדו. והיה בטחונו באריכות ימיו בעולם סבה לארך תאותו בעניניו וסבה לקצר תאותו בעניני אחריתו.

וכאשר יוכיחנו מוכיח ויורנו מורה ויאמר לו עד מתי אתה מתעלם מחשב בצידתך וענייני בית מועדך

יאמר עד שיהיה לי די פרנסתי וספוקי ולכל אשר אתי מאשה ובנים עד סוף ימינו תנוח נפשי מדאגות העולם ואפנה לפרע חובותי לבורא ואחשב בסבות הצידה ליום המועד.

~~ פרק ו ~~
וראיתי להראות פני סכלותם וטעותם בדעת הזאת בשבעה ענינים אגלה בהם גדל טעותם ואם יארכו דברינו בעבור שיש בזה מן הביוש והתוכחת לבעלי הדעה הזאת

והם כת בעלי המשכונות ענינם בזה כענין הסוחר שהוא מוכר באשראי למי שאינו מאמינו וימשכנהו בעת המכר מפני יראתו ממעוט אמונתו ושלא תמצא ידו לפרעו.

והראשון מאפני התשובה עליו שנאמר לו אתה האיש המסתפק בגזרת הבורא ושאיננו מאמין בגדל עצמתו אשר חשך אור שכלו וכבה נר תבונתו בגבר אפלת תאותו עליו הטוב לך לבקש משכון ולקחתו אלא

37

מרעך וחברך אשר אין לו רשות עליך ולא מצותו עוברת עליך. אבל השכיר כשהוא משתכר אצל בני אדם אין טוב למשכן שוכרו בשכרו קדם עבודתו וכל שכן העבד שלא ימשכן אדוניו קדם עבודתו לו בפרנסתו קל וחומר הנוצר שלא ימשכן יוצרו קדם עבודתו לו.

ומן התמה כי עבודת העבד לאדוניו על מנת שיפרע לו שכרו אחר עבודתו גנאי הוא כמו שאמרו (משנה אבות א ג) אל תהיו כעבדים המשמשים את הרב על מנת לקבל פרס וכו' כל שכן שיעז פניו לבקש משכון בפרנסתו קדם עבודתו. ובדומה לזה אמר הכתוב (דברים לב ו) אל תהיו כעבדים המשמשים את הרב על מנת לקבל פרס וכו'.

והשני שכל המקבל משכון מחברו יש לו קצבה ולבקשתו תכלה אך בעל הדעת הזאת אין לו קץ לבקשתו כי אינו יודע מה יספיק לפרנסתו ופרנסת אנשי ביתו ממזון ומותרים עד יום מותם. ואילו היה לו ממון כפלי כפלים ממה שיספיק לו לא תנוח נפשו מפני שקצם נעלם ומדת ימיהם אינה ידועה והוא סכל במה שבקש מפני שאין לו תכלית אצלו ולא שעור.

והשלישי שהממשכן את חברו איננו ממשכן אותו אלא אם לא קדם לו חוב שהוא חיב בו ואינו משה בו משאת מאומה והדין עמו. אבל אם קדמו לחברו עליו חובות שהוא חיב בהם וידע שיש לו עליו חובות ראויים אין לו לבקש ממנו משכון בשום פנים ולא יהיה ראוי לקחתו ממנו אפלו אם יתנדב בו הממשכן.

כל שכן הבורא שיש לו על האדם מן החובות הראויים מה שאלו היו מקבצים מעשי כל בני אדם בכל ימות העולם לאיש אחד מהם לא היה מספיק הכל לגמל טובה אחת מטובות הבורא עליו.

ואיך לא יתביש זה העז פנים לבקש מן הבורא שיקדים טובות גדולות על מה שקדם לו אצלו ויכבד החוב עליו ושמא לא ישלם לו מה שנדר לו מן העבודה בעבור כלות ימיו ובוא קצו.

והיה אחד מן החסידים אומר לבני אדם בני אדם! היתכן שיתבע אתכם הבורא בחובות מחרת ביום הזה וכן במה שאתם חייבים אחריו בשנה ושנים?

אמרו לו היאך יתכן שנהיה נתבעים בחובות הימים שאין אנו יודעין אם נחיה עד שנגיע אליהם ויחייבונו בהם. אבל אנו חיבים עבודה ידועה בזמן ידוע וכאשר נגיע לזמן נתחיב בעבודה.

אמר להם וכן ערב לכם הבורא יתברך לכל זמן ידוע טרף ידוע ועליכם בו עבודה קבועה וכאשר איננו תובע אתכם בעבודה קודם עתה כן ראוי שיהיה בפניכם בשת תמנע אתכם מלבקש טרף שלא הגיע עתו. ומדוע אני רואה אתכם מבקשים ממנו טרפי שנים באות אינכם יודעים אם ימיכם יגיעו אליהם ותבקשו להקדים לכם טרף מי שלא נברא עדיין מאשה ובנים. ולא יספיק לכם המזון לבדו אלא שאתם מקדימים המזון ומותריו לזמנים שאינם ידועים ולא ערובים לכם. ולא די לכם שאינכם מקדימים לו עבודה לזמן עתיד אלא שאינכם מחשבים עם נפשותיכם במה שהתעלמתם מן העבודה במה שעברו מן הימים אשר לא התעלם מהשלים לכם טרפם בם.

והרביעי כי הממשכן את חברו הוא ממשכן אותו לאחת משלש עלות אחת מהן שמא יעני ולא תשיג ידו. והשנית שמא יקפץ ידו על מה שיש אצלו ולא יוכל להפרע ממנו. והשלישית מפני שהוא ירא שמא ימות או שלא ימצאהו. והמשכון רפואת המדוים האלה בין בני אדם. ואלו היו בטוחים בני אדם קצתם בקצתם מאלה השלש מדות היה גנאי להם למשכן מבלי ספק. והבורא יתברך אשר לא יאותו לו אלו המדות יותר הוא גנאי גדול ומפלא שימשכנו אותו וכבר אמר הכתוב (חגי ב ח) לי הכסף ולי הזהב וגו', ואמר (דברי הימים א כט יב) והעשר והכבוד מלפניך.

והחמישי כי הממשכן את חברו תנוח נפשו במשכון מפני שהוא מקוה להפרע ממנו ולהנות בו או בתמורתו. אבל מי שיחשב כי כאשר יקדים לו הבורא די שפקו תנוח נפשו מצד העולם טענתו שקר מפני שאיננו בטוח בהשאר הממון אצלו שאפשר שיקרהו פגע מן הפגעים המבדילים בינו לבינו כמו שאמר הכתוב (ירמיה יז יא) בחצי ימיו יעזבנו.

ומה שטענו ממנוחת נפשם בהגיעם אל חפצם מהון העולם כזב וסכלות מהם בבקשותם כי אפשר שיהיה סבה חזקה לטרדת לבם ולצער נפשם כמו שאמרו רבותינו זכרונם לברכה (משנה אבות ב ז) מרבה נכסים מרבה דאגה.

והששי כי המקבל משכון מחברו אלו היה ברור לו שיפרעהו קדם זמנו ויגמלהו תחת המתנתו כפל מה שיש לו אצלו לחסד עליו לא היה ממשכן אותו בשום פנים. והבורא יתברך אשר ידענו מנהגו הטוב עמנו וטובו הגדול עלינו חדשים גם ישנים ושהוא גומל על מעשה הצדקה והעבודה במה שאינו עולה בדעת כל שכן שיספר כמו שכתוב (ישעיה סד ג) עין לא ראתה אלהים זולתך יעשה למחכה לו, יותר הוא גנאי גדול שנמשכן

אותו.

והשביעי כי הממשכן את חברו אינו ממשכנו אלא אחר שהוא יכול
למלאת מה שממשכנו בעבורו מהון העולם אבל הממשכן הבורא יתברך
בהקדמת הטובות אליו אין לו יכלת לשלם העבודה עליהן ולא מבטח
לפרע מה שיש עליו מן החובות הישנות כל שכן החדשות שהאדם
הצדיק איננו פורע חובות טובת האלהים עליו אלא בעזר האלהים לו כמו
שאמר אחד מן החסידים בתשבחותיו ואף המשכיל היודע אותך לא
במעשהו יתהלל כי אם בשמך וברחמיך אשר הכינות את לבבו לדעת
אותך כי בך יצדקו ויתהללו כל זרע ישראל לאמר (תהלים מד ט) באלהים
הללנו כל היום וגו'.

~~ פרק ז ~~

וכיון שהשלמנו בשער הזה מה שהיה ראוי לו מן הדברים כפי השגתנו
ראוי לנו עתה לבאר מפסידי הבטחון באלהים. ואמר כי מפסידי שלשת
השערים הקודמים בספר הזה כלם מפסידים הבטחון.

ומפסידיו עוד:

הסכלות בענין הבורא ובמדותיו הטובות כי מי שאינו מבין רחמי הבורא
על ברואיו והגנתו עליהם והשגחתו ומשלו בהם ושהם קשורים באסוריו
לא ינוח לבו ולא יסמך עליו.

ומהם סכלותו במצות הבורא יתברך רצוני לומר תורתו אשר הזהיר בה
לסמך עליו ולבטח בו כמו שאמר (מלאכי ג י) ובחנוני נא בזאת, ואמר
(ישעיה כו ד) בטחו בה' עדי עד.

ומהם נטותו אל הסבות הקרובות אשר הוא רואה אותן ולא ידע כי
העלות כל אשר תקרבנה מהמעולל תמעט יכלתם להועיל למעולל
ולהזיקו. וכל אשר תרחקנה יהיה כח יכלתם להועילו ולהזיקו יותר חזק
ונראה.

כמו המלך כשהוא רוצה לענות אחד מעבדיו מצוה משנהו לעשות
והמשנה מצוה השר והשר מצוה השוטר והשוטר מצוה לסרדיוט
והסרדיוט מצוה הנוגשים והנוגשים מקימים המעשה בכלים מוכנים לו.

ואשר יכלתו מעוטה מכלם להקל מצערו ולהוסיף עליו הם הכלים מפני
שאין להם חפץ והנוגשים יותר יכולים מהכלים וכן הסרדיוט יותר

מהנוגשים והשוטר יותר מן הסרדיוט והשר יותר מן השוטר והמשנה יותר מהשר והמלך יותר מכלם מפני שאם ירצה ימחל לו.

וכבר נראה לך כי חלישות העלות וחזקתם להועיל למעולל תהיינה כפי קרבתם ורחקם ממנו. והבורא יתעלה אשר הוא תכלית העלות ברחק מן המעוללים ראוי לבטח בו ולסמך עליו לחזק יכלתו על תועלתם ונזקם כאשר קדמנו מן הדברים.

וכללו של דבר בענין הבטחון כי יתרון הבטחון מהבוטחים באלהים כפי יתרון ידיעתם אותו ואמונתם בהגנתו עליהם ורוב השגחתו על טובתם.

והנה הילד בתחלת ענינו בוטח על שדי אמו כמו שנאמר (תהלים כב י) מבטיחי על שדי אמי. וכאשר תחזק הכרתו משיב בטחונו על אמו לרוב השגחתה עליו כמו שנאמר (תהלים קלא ב) אם לא שויתי ודוממתי נפשי כגמול עלי אמו וגו'. וכשתתחזק הכרתו עוד ורואה כי הנהגת אמו אל אביו משיב בטחונו אליו למעלת הגנתו עליו. וכאשר יחזק גופו ותתכן לו תחבולה במחיתו במלאכה או סחורה והדומה להם משיב בטחונו אל כחו ותחבולתו מפני סכלותו בכל אשר קדם בטובת הנהגת האלהים.

ואמרו על אחד מן החסידים שהיה לו שכן סופר מהיר והיה מתפרנס משכר ספרותו. אמר לו יום אחד היאך ענינך, אמר לו בטוב בעוד ידי שלמה. ולערב היום ההוא נגדעה ידו ולא כתב בה כל שאר ימיו והיה זה ענשו מהאל יתברך על אשר בטח על ידו.

ואם יתכן לו טרפו על ידי זולתו מן הבריות ישיב בטחונו אליהם ותנוח נפשו עליהם.

וכשתתחזק הכרתו ויראה חסרונם וצרכם אל הבורא יתברך ישיב בטחונו אליו ויסמך עליו בענינים שאין לו יכלת בהם ולא יוכל להמלט מהמסר בם אל גזרת הבורא כמו ירידת הגשמים על הזריעה והליכת הים והליכת המדברות מאין מים ובבוא שטף ובנפל הדבר בחיים והדומה לזה מן הענינים אשר אין בהם לאדם שום תחבולה בשום פנים כמו שנאמר (ירמיה ב כז) ובעת רעתם יאמרו קומה והושיענו.

ואם תחזק הכרתו באלהים עוד יבטח בו גם כן במה שיתכן לו בו בו קצת תחבולה כמו הבאת הטרף בסבות המסכנות והמלאכות המיגעות את הגופים ויניח לבטחונו באלהים שיטריפהו במה שיהיה קל להתעסק בו יותר מהן.

41

ואם תחזק הכרתו באלהים יותר ישיב בטחונו אליו בכל הסבות הקשה מהן והקלה ויכון בהתעסקו בהן לעבודת האלהים ולשמר מצוותיו.

וכאשר תחזק הכרתו יותר מזה בחמלת הבורא על ברואיו ירצה במה שיהיה מגזרת האלהים לו בלבו ובלשונו ובנראהו ובנסתרו וישמח בכל אשר עשה לו האלהים ממות וחיים וריש ועשר ובריאות וחלי לא יכסף לזולת מה שבחר לו האלהים ולא ירצה אלא מה שרצה לו

ונמסר אל האלהים ומשליך נפשו וגופו אל דינו. ולא יגביר ענין על ענין ולא יבחר זולת מה שהוא בו מעניני עולמו כמו שאמר אחד מן הבוטחים לא השכמתי מעולם בענין והתאויתי לזולתו.

וכאשר תחזק הכרתו באלהים יותר מזה וידע הענין המכון אליו בבריאתו ויציאתו אל העולם הזה הכלה ויכיר מעלת העולם האחר הקים ימאס בעולם הזה ובסבותיו וימסר במחשבתו ובנפשו וגופו אל האלהים יתברך וישתעשע בזכרו בבדידות וישתומם מבלתי המחשבה בגדלתו.

ואם יהיה במקהלות לא יתאוה כי אם לרצונו ולא יכסף כי אם לפגיעתו ותטרידהו שמחתו באהבתו משמחת אנשי העולם בעולם ושמחת אנשי העולם הבא בעולם הבא.

וזאת העליונה שבמדרגות הבוטחים מהנביאים וחסידים וסגלת האלהים הזכים והוא מה שאמר הכתוב (ישעיה כו ח) אף ארח משפטיך ה' קוינוך לשמך ולזכרך תאות נפש, ואמר (תהלים מב ג) צמאה נפשי לאלהים לאל חי.

אלה עשר מדרגות הבטחון אשר לא ימלט בוטח מאחת מהנה. ומצאנו ענין הבטחון בלשון הקודש מליצים בעדו בעשר מלות כנגד עשר מדרגות האלה והן

מבטח, ומשען, ותקוה, ומחסה, ותוחלת, וחכוי, וסמיכה, ושבר, ומסעד, וכסל.

האלהים ישימנו מן הבוטחים עליו הנמסרים לדינו בנראה ובנסתר ברחמיו אמן

נשלם שער הבטחון לאל אחרון וראשון.